MATHEMATICS AND THE STUDY OF SOCIAL RELATIONS

Patrick Doreian

Lecturer in Sociology
University of Essex

WEIDENFELD AND NICOLSON
5 Winsley Street London W1

SBN 297 00240 6

Printed in Great Britain by
C. Tinling & Co. Ltd, London and Prescot

Preface

The use of mathematics in sociology is continually increasing and there is, therefore, a growing need for an understanding of mathematics to become more widespread in the discipline. This is especially the case if the dogmatic extremes of trying to exclude mathematics completely on the one hand, and attempting to mathematise everything on the other, are to be avoided.

In teaching courses on mathematical sociology, I have frequently found that the material I want to draw on is scattered in a variety of places. There is the need, therefore, to draw these together and provide an introduction to them. I also want to point out particular growth points in the discipline where mathematics may prove useful.

With these three objectives I have been led to be extremely selective over the sociological topics considered and the mathematics employed. Because of the introductory nature of the book I have chosen to emphasise sociological issues rather than mathematical techniques. In this respect the book is much like a review of part of the literature.

I have included enough mathematics to make the book reasonably self-sufficient. However, it is important that the reader goes beyond the book, both with respect to sociological issues and an understanding of mathematics. I have excluded probability theory although a large part of the use of mathematics in sociology rests on an understanding of probability. This is particularly true of the use of statistics for data analysis and the use of causal models. For excellent introductions in these areas the reader is referred to Blalock (1960, 1964, 1969). Stochastic models have had to be excluded also (although in considering social mobility I have included a section using them). For stochastic models the work of Bartos (1967) and Coleman (1964) can be profitably read. Finally, for the reader who wants a better understanding of mathematics, the introductory texts of McGinnis (1965) and Kemeny, Snell and Thompson (1957) are highly recommended.

The basic tools used in this book are those of set theory which are introduced in Chapter 2. Parts of this chapter can be missed on a first reading. (I have adopted the notation throughout the book of marking such passages with an asterisk.) The topics in the succeeding chapters follow quite naturally from Chapter 2, particularly from the concept of a relation. Also I start with what might be considered micro-sociology (Chapter 4) and gradually broaden the scope in successive chapters (5–8). Chapters 3 and 9 are devoted to the broad problems of measurement and mathematical sociology respectively.

My thanks go first and foremost to those authors whose work I have drawn on for the intellectual stimulation their writing has given me. Tony Coxon, Geoffrey Hawthorn and Norman Stockman read through the entire manuscript offering many helpful comments and corrections. Other colleagues, notably Peter Abell, have given me help and encouragement. My gratitude is due also to Dr Peter Chapman, without whose help I would never have completed the manuscript, and Marion Haberhauer for the excellence of her secretarial assistance.

University of Essex   Patrick Doreian

Contents

Contents

1. Introduction

Every day we, as individuals, observe social life. More accurately, we observe a sample of the life going on around us, which is a tiny part of social life. Nevertheless we often make assumptions, from this (biased) sample, about individuals or society in general. Daily we assume at least a minimal amount of common understanding with the people around us, we have expectations concerning their behaviour, and act accordingly. Our vocabulary, however limited, is usually sufficient for this. Sociologists, and social scientists generally, have studied the same social life using techniques and terminology that are radically different from those of the so-called man in the street. Canons of procedure and criteria for assessing the result of this enquiry are adopted. In the light of these the work of particular sociologists can be evaluated.

However, this is an ideal and there are many differences of opinion among sociologists as to what social theory is, what the appropriate methodologies are and what the end product, sociology, ought to be. While this diversity can be stimulating, it is unfortunate that a considerable part of the sociological literature, and presumably of sociologists' time, is taken up with disputes as to which 'perspective' is the correct one. In view of these differences, it is necessary at the outset to describe very briefly the view I take of sociology and the place of mathematics in the subject.

1.1 On Social Theory
Without a conceptual framework of some sort, it is impossible to study social life or, indeed, anything. Strictly speaking, these

A*

frameworks are arbitrary in the sense that we are not in the position to say which set of concepts are the correct ones. Our choices of concepts and theories are based on criteria of fruitfulness and our understanding of explanation. To the extent that values are involved in the choice of subjects for study and the way in which these are pursued, there can be no value-free sociology.[1] Objective criteria and canons of procedure are only objective in the relative sense that a group of theorists abide by them.

We have in the first instance to decide what we are studying and then how we go about it. These problems and procedures are outlined by concepts, and sociologists differ in their choice of these. We often start by specifying units of analysis which are basically the social objects we study. Clearly people (as individuals) constitute one such unit of analysis. Now people do not act independently of each other all of the time – they may behave without regard for each other, but that is a different matter. Groups of people are another unit of analysis. In general terms we can take social organisation to be a process whereby order and meaning are given to social life[2] (Olsen, 1968). There are many forms of social organisation, and these too can be units of analysis. They are manifold and include families, kinship groups, networks, associations, formal organisations, social classes, aggregates, communities and even societies.

By considering the constraints on the behaviour of an individual, further units of analysis can be outlined. For example, in a given situation he finds that people have definite expectations of his behaviour. He has a role, and people around him have sanctions they can apply in an attempt to make his behaviour conform to their expectations. It is possible to regard roles, values, norms and sanctions also as units of analysis. Some theorists have consequently distinguished different levels of analysis; cultural, social, personality (as well as an organic level)[3] and, while these are not independent of each other, sociological analysis is generally confined to the social level. (See the references for a discussion of this.)

Given that there are many available units of analysis, it is not surprising that we frequently need to consider different units of analysis simultaneously (and also move from one level of analysis to another). For example, an individual belongs to a group in a formal organisation and we need to be able to move freely from one unit to another in order to be able to relate these units. Some social theorists are concerned that these units of analysis are too close to intuitively obvious notions about people (and the groups to which they belong) to be scientifically useful. Such a theorist would feel it necessary to establish theoretical concepts that are not empirically obvious and not ambiguous. Role, rather than person, is such a concept and a role structure rather than a collection of individuals is another. It is unlikely that conversational concepts will be theoretically the most relevant. However, in the course of this book I shall use both conversational and theoretical concepts, although the latter are more important.

In a particular study we need to specify the kind of unit of analysis and then to specify clearly and unambiguously what the population of a study is. For example, we may decide to study individuals in, say, a particular rural area. If the results are not meant to be generalised beyond the particular population in a given rural area, this has to be clearly stated. Having delineated units of analysis, we need to describe those properties we are concerned with. In this sense the behaviour of these units will be one of these properties. Concepts that delineate these properties (or attributes) are called variables. For example, if a unit of analysis is a small group, the variables cohesiveness and integration can be used to describe the group. The relations between the individuals in the group can be described in terms of variables like amount of interaction, and variables can also be used to characterise the individuals of the group.

A scientific proposition is simply a statement relating two or more variables to each other which can meaningfully be said to be true or false. A theory is then a set of inter-related propositions. It is clear that as both the variables and the relations between them are specified by concepts, the theory is also. Sociological theory has as its objective the determination of regularities of social phenomena, the establishment of general laws and, on the basis of these laws, the explanation and prediction of social phenomena.[4] Alternatively, we can regard this as an analysis of the causes and effects of social phenomena.

There are, however, many different and competing sociological theories. It is possible that social phenomena explained by one theory cannot be explained by another. A theory may provide a spurious explanation and two (distinct) theories may individually only partially explain a social phenomenon. Furthermore, two theories may explain a particular social phenomena but use completely different variables in doing so while two theories may provide contradictory explanations. In all such cases we have to assess the relative merits of, and the differences between, the theories involved. However, before this can be done we need to check whether different theorists are using the same or different concepts and also whether they are referring to the same or different phenomena. The choice of concepts in a particular theory should be made deliberately, although frequently it is done by default. On top of this, the same concept is frequently defined quite differently in different contexts.

Theories relate variables to each other and frequently these variables are not directly observable. However, in order to test such a theory we need to be able to relate the theoretical concepts to what is observed. It is in this context that the distinction between observational and theoretical concepts is made (see Torgerson, 1958). For each theoretical concept there is at least one corresponding observational concept. Such observational concepts are called *indicators* of the appropriate theoretical concept. The place and role of indicators in the social sciences is the topic of a continuing debate. (See, for example, Hempel (1952), Lazarsfeld (1959) and Costner (1969), Blalock (1969).) Frequently an investigator guesses the indicators of a particular theoretical concept. This leaves the relation between

a concept and its indicators unspecified. This has led to a particular observational concept (for example, occupation) being
taken as an instance of more than one theoretical concept (for
example, class, status and prestige). Where there is little consensus on the appropriate indicators, or where the relation between
theoretical concepts and their corresponding indicators is
simply assumed to be unproblematical, controversies over the
meaning of variables abound.

However, while it may be useful to distinguish analytically
between theoretical and observational concepts, the distinction
is less easy to make in reality. Empirical procedures, particularly measurement, must be considered when theory is being
constructed. Frequently the most elementary procedures are
based on theoretical considerations, and there is an inevitable
confusion of the two types of concepts (see Blalock and Blalock,
Ch. 1, 1968).

Especially as different sociologists have different perspec-
tives, employ different concepts, and produce different, even
contradictory, explanations of social phenomena, it is crucial
that they be able to communicate with one another. Such
communication should lead (according to favourable accounts
of scientific activity) to a progressive refinement of concepts.
Even though this refinement does not always occur, concepts
do need to be used with precision and not as convenient
receptacles into which many meanings can be poured. We may
lose some literary elegance, or rather flamboyance, as a result,
but a continued use of allusions to convey vagueness is an abuse
of language rather than a display of its richness, especially
when one is attempting to explain something.

1.2 Mathematics and Sociology

Mathematics is frequently taken to be dry, dull and beyond
argument. Contrary to current stereotypes of the subject,
mathematics is a very rich and creative discipline. It is far from
dead and the rate of growth is accelerating. These are two
bold assertions – but see Wilder (1968), Kline (1952) and an

excellent selection of readings (Kline (ed.), 1969) for evidence of this.

At first sight, it would appear that mathematics is concerned with abstract relations and social theory with empirical social relations. However, the concepts of social theory are abstractions also, and there is no intrinsic reason why mathematics cannot be used to express theoretical, or even empirical, statements.

This is, of course, to overstate my case. Such a sweeping statement cannot be disproved (and in defending it I could always point to the future). However, this would gloss over the fact that not all attempts to use mathematics in the social sciences, and the natural sciences for that matter, have met with success, instant or otherwise. The decision to use or not to use a particular part of mathematics is an empirical decision that can only be made in the light of what the problem is, what the role of mathematics is in the problem and how much success is gained from using mathematics. Among the possible benefits of having a mathematical statement of theories is that generalisation is immediately and legitimately available. The use of mathematics can lead to the finding of significant results simply because of the deductive fertility of mathematics. These results may have been difficult, or even impossible, to establish in a verbal formulation. In order for this to occur, our concepts (of social objects and relations) must be precise. A chameleon concept with many shades of meaning may be useful as a summary concept, but it is a liability when hypotheses and testable relations are being explored. Greater precision is regarded as one of the advantages gained through using mathematics but it does not follow that precision can only be achieved through using mathematics. Furthermore, some sociologists would claim that the precision gained through the use of mathematics is bought at too high a price: trivialisation of the sociological problems considered. In practice, this has frequently been the case but, ultimately, triviality lies in the continued use of ambiguous concepts. Ambiguous social theory cannot be realistically debated nor meaningfully extended.

The paucity of measurement models is often cited as a reason why there is no place for mathematics in sociology. However, such an argument is misconstrued; as the simple labelling of social objects is a form of measurement and without any terms at all, sociology – and discussion – are impossible. Even the simple dichotomy gives a genuine measurement system and all social phenomena can, in principle, be measured. What is really at issue is the level of measurement and my contention is that there is only one context in which measurement properties can be discussed; mathematics. This line of reasoning also points out that the dichotomy of qualitative versus quantitative analysis is not only overworked but can even be misleading.

Given that every theoretical statement in sociology (when tested) is based on some form of measurement, it is erroneous to insist that only mathematically inclined sociologists have the responsibility to establish measurement properties. It is also erroneous to equate the application of mathematics with quantification. In fact, much of this book is concerned with so-called qualitative analysis. Coombs (1964), Coleman (1964) and others have repeatedly stressed the need for theoretical statements to give the *form* of a relationship as well as stating the existence of a relationship. The conditions for this, however, need careful discussion and the problem is taken up in the chapter on measurement and in the final chapter.

2. Relations

If sociological theory can be regarded as a collection of inter-related and logically consistent propositions, then these propositions, individually and collectively, express our understanding of social phenomena by relating certain variables to each other. Furthermore, I would contend that for the sociologist the phenomena he studies consist mainly of social objects and social relations holding between those objects. Both of the terms 'variable' and 'relation' are ubiquitous in sociology and because they can be defined as particular sets they can be given a precise definition. The definition that is given in the course of this chapter is very important, not only because this book is about social relations, but also because it can be used to define the notion of structure (see Chapter 4). For readers who are not familiar with set theory this chapter will probably have to be taken quite slowly. However, once mastered, set theory provides a very simple and efficient means of dealing with various concepts and both of the notions of mapping and homomorphism are crucial for the discussion of measurement (Chapter 3) and status (Chapter 7).

2.1 Elements and Sets

Any collection of objects that is well defined – in the sense defined below – is a set, and the objects making up a set are called the elements of that set. Both these terms are undefined beyond this, they are primitive notions. The following are all examples of sets:

(i) Men with fluorescent green shirts.

(ii) All people living in a particular community.

(iii) London, Paris, Rome.

(iv) Pork pie, prostitute, pauper.

(v) All countries with a totalitarian regime.

(vi) The respondents of a particular survey sample.

It is precisely because the terms 'set' and 'element' are primitive notions that we are able to talk about sets in general without having always to refer to a particular context. The operations that are defined in the next section apply to *all* sets that are *well-defined*. But first we need to take a closer look at our six xeamples. Mathematicians might have some qualms over accepting them as sets, and their uneasiness would stem from the requirement that sets be well defined. This means that there is no ambiguity about the set; it is made up of certain elements and no others.

Before proceeding further, it is helpful to establish a notation. Elements will always be denoted by lower-case letters and sets by capital letters. Brackets, { }, will also be used to denote sets when they are written out or defined in a certain way. Sets can be defined by listing all the elements. For example:

$$\{0, 1, 2, 3, 4, 5, 6, 7, 8, 9\}$$

is a set that is defined in this manner just as {London, Paris, Rome} is such a set. This is a definition *by extension*. Alternatively, a set can be defined by specifying a property that characterises all the elements of the set:

$$A = \{a | a \text{ has the property } P\}$$

which is read: '*A* is the set of all those elements *a* such that *a* is characterised by *P*'. This is a definition *by intension*. Of the examples of sets given earlier, (i), (ii), (v) and (vi) are written in this way. For a particular element, say *a*, and a given set *A*, the element either belongs to *A* or it does not belong to *A*. These two states of affairs are denoted respectively by $a \in A$ and $a \notin A$ (where $\in$ denotes 'is an element of' and $\notin$ denotes 'is not an element of').

Can the 'set', $A = \{a|a$ is a person resident in Britain$\}$ be a meaningful legitimate set? There are two problems to consider. One concerns what we mean by the various terms and the other with the permanence[1] of sets. It is irrelevant here to give a definition of person, or of resident in (for example, a sociologist may be interested in people over 21 who spend so many months in every year in Britain). What matters is whether or not definitions can be made.[2] If no definitions are possible, or if many collections satisfy one definition, then quite literally we do not know what we are talking about.

If every element of a set X is also an element of a set Y then X is called a *subset* of Y. This is denoted by $X \subset Y$ which is read as 'X is strictly a subset of Y', or 'X is a set strictly contained in Y'. If there is one element of Y that is not in X then X is a strict subset of Y. Thus of the set $\{$London, Rome, Paris$\}$ the set $\{$London, Paris$\}$ is a subset. In this sense, a set cannot be a subset of itself. If we allow a set to be a subset of itself we use the notation $X \subseteq Y$. The empty set, denoted by ϕ, contains no elements and is a subset of all sets. All the subsets of a set Y, excluding the set itself and ϕ, are called the proper subsets of Y. Two sets are equal if and only if they each contain the same elements. If X and Y are equal, this is denoted by $X = Y$ and if they are not equal, we have $X \neq Y$. Thus another way of defining $X \subset Y$ is $(X \subseteq Y$ and $X \neq Y)$.

Suppose now that we have (i) a set $S = \{s_i\}$ of elements, s_i, (ii) there is a finite number n of the s_i,[3] and (iii) (at least) some elements can be distinguished from one another in terms of a specified property. Such a set is then termed a *variable*. Stated as such, a variable is an unspecified subset of S, although a variable can be taken as the whole set (in which case all the elements will be distinguished from one another in terms of the property being used). Let $S = \{$under 18 years, 18–20, 21–35, 35–50, over 50$\} = \{s_i\}$, then S is the variable 'age' and s_i can denote any one of the elements of S, which in this example are age groups.[4] Similarly, if $S = \{$male, female$\}$ we have the variable 'sex' and s_i can denote either of the elements of S. Each element of a variable is called a value (of that variable).

2.2 Basic Set Operations

If we have a collection of sets, then we can transform one or some of these into other sets. We do this by means of operations. Given an initial set, or sets, each operation creates a unique set from them. (These operations can be represented diagrammatically in Venn diagrams where an enclosed area represents a set. Figure 2.1 shows a Venn diagram for each operation presented here.)

The *union* of two sets is a set that contains all the elements in the original two sets. This operation (of union) is denoted by $\cup$ and for two sets A and B,

$$A \cup B = \{a | a \in A \text{ or } a \in B\}$$

If there are elements common to both of the sets, A and B, these elements appear only once in the union of A and B. If $A = \{a | a \text{ is a person over 16 and under 25}\}$ and $B = \{b | b \text{ is a person over 21 and under 30}\}$ then $A \cup B = \{a | a \text{ is a person over 16 and under 30}\}$.[5] Given the sets A and B, their union $(A \cup B)$ is unique, however the set $A \cup B$ can be constructed from many other sets. For example, if $A_1 = \{a | a \text{ is a person over 16 and under 20}\}$ and $B_1 = \{b | b \text{ is a person over 18 and under 30}\}$, $A_1 \cup B_1 = A \cup B$.

The *intersection* of two sets contains only those elements that belong to both of the sets and the operation is denoted by $\cap$. If A and B are two sets then $A \cap B = \{a | a \in A \text{ and } a \in B\}$. In terms of the examples in the previous paragraph, $A \cap B = \{a | a \text{ is a person over 21 and under 25}\}$ and $A_1 \cap B_1 = \}a | a \text{ is a person over 18 and under 21}\}$.

Two sets are *disjoint* (or mutually exclusive) if their intersection is the empty set. For a set we can define the *universe* or universal set U. The universal set is not unique but it specifies those elements that can belong to sets in a particular area of discussion. The notion is naturally illustrated by the sociological example where the population under study (for example, youth in a town, people in a high-rise development, inmates in a prison) is the universe and all the subsets of U are possible samples. If we have a sample of youths we could, say, determine their average age. We could do this for all possible samples and so construct the sampling distribution (in this case). For a set S the set of all subsets is called the *power set* of S. If there are n elements in S there are 2^n possible subsets.

The *complement* of a set A are those elements that are in the universe but not in the set A. This set is denoted by A'; $A' = \{a|a \notin A$ and $a \in U\}$. Continuing our example, if U is the set of all people, then $A' = \{a|a$ is a person under (or equal to) 16 and over (or equal to) 25$\}$. If the universe was the set of all people over 16, then in this universe $A' = \{a|a$ is over (or equal to) 25$\}$.

Two other operations are the *difference* of two sets and the *symmetric difference* of two sets. If A and B are two sets then the difference $A - B = \{a|a \in A$ and $a \notin B\}$. This set is obtained simply by removing from A those elements that are also in B. It is easily shown that $A - B = A \cap B'$ (those elements that are in A and also in B') and that this operation can be defined in terms of two previous operations. The symmetric difference of A and B is the set $\{a|a \in A - B$ or $a \in B - A\}$ and we denote this by $A \oplus B$. It is easily demonstrated that $A \oplus B$ is the complement of $A \cap B$ in the universe $A \cup B$.

* These operations satisfy many equations, some of which are given in Appendix A. At this point, four such equations can be briefly mentioned. The union operation satisfies:

(i) $A \cup B = B \cup A$ (commutative law)
(ii) $A \subseteq A \cup B, B \subseteq A \cup B$
(iii) $A \cap B \subseteq B, A \cap B \subseteq A$
(iv) $A \cup (B \cup C) = (A \cup B) \cup C$ (associative law)

The fourth of these equations indicates that in forming the union of three sets, the order in which we proceed is immaterial. We can form the union of any number of sets:

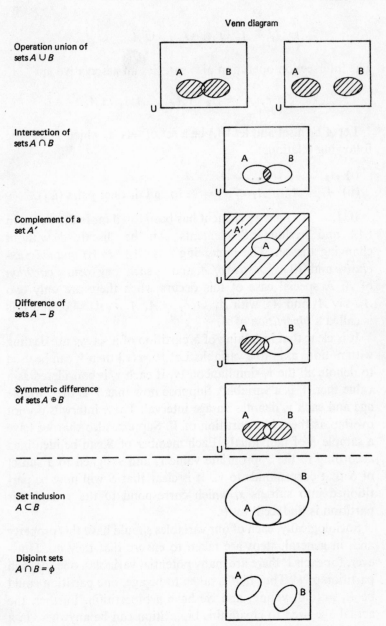

Figure 2.1 Venn diagram for set theoretic operations

$$\bigcup_{i=1}^{n} A_i = A_1 \cup A_2 \cup \ldots \cup A_{n-1} \cup A_n.$$

The intersection operation also satisfies an associative law;

$$\bigcap_{i=1}^{n} A_i = A_1 \cap A_2 \ldots A_{n-1} \cap A_n.$$

Let A be a set and let $\{A_i\}$ be a set of sets A_i which satisfy the following relations:

(i) $A_1 \cup A_2 \cup \ldots \cup A_n = A$

(ii) $A_i = A_j$ or $A_i \cap A_j = \phi$, for all distinct pairs (i, j)

If $A_i = A_j$, then an element has been listed more than once in $\{A_i\}$ and 'redundant' elements can be discarded without changing the set. The remaining sets $\{A_i\}$ are (i) *mutually exclusive* and (ii) *exhaustive of A*, and as such they form a *partition* of A. A special case of this occurs when there are only two A_i, say A_1 and A_2, with $A_1 \cup A_2 = A$, $A_1 \cap A_2 = \phi$, and this is called a *bipartition* of A.

It is clear that in talking of a partition of a set we are dealing with notions akin to a variable. Let $V = \{v_i\}$ then V can be used to denote all the v_i simultaneously. If each v_i is considered as a value then V is a variable[6]. Suppose now that V is the variable age and each v_i denotes an age interval. These intervals do not overlap as there is a partition of V. Suppose also that we have a sample S of individuals. Each member of S can be identified according to the appropriate value v_i and assigned to a subset of S that corresponds to v_i. It is clear that S will now be partitioned into subsets s_i which correspond to the v_i and this partition is 'induced' by V.

Sociologically, each of our variables should have this property and, in general, steps are taken to ensure that they do. However, for each V there are many potential variables, one for each partition of V. Thus if V is taken to be age, one partition could be $V_1 = \{$old, young$\}$ and we have a bipartition. Further, the actual age used to create this bipartition can be anywhere in a specified age range. Another partition V_2 could be into ten year age intervals and yet another partition V_3 could have a value v_i for each year of a specified age range. These different partitions are not totally disparate and there can be some control over which one is considered. Thus if we form unions of values of V_3 we can create V_2 and this is nothing more than collapsing the categories of a variable. Similarly, V_3 could be collapsed into V_1. The partition V_2 may or may not yield V_1 through successive unions of values. If the age that divides S into the old and the young is an element of one of the values of V_2 then V_2 cannot be collapsed to V_1.

For many variables a partition is constructed by taking all the values v_i used, forming $\cup_i\{v_i\} = V$ and then finding V' in the appropriate universal set. This is nothing more than a residual category. However, we need to ask if V' (which is a set) is well-defined. Thus if R (religion) = {protestant, catholic, other} is a variable and if the element s_i of the partition of S corresponding to 'other' is large and denotes more than one other religion, then the residual category is unlikely to be useful (for sociological purposes).

Categories for analysis are created through intersections of variables. For two variables (which are each bipartitions and induce bipartitions of S), the intersection can be formed which will result in the familiar 2×2 contingency table. Clearly we can do the same if the variables are partitions and so obtain a larger contingency table[7]. This procedure is not limited to two variables, the only constraints being comprehension and practical computation. By attempting to consider two variables simultaneously we are led naturally to consider relations.

2.3 Relations

When a listing of the elements of a set is given, the order in which these elements are written is irrelevant. The set {a, b} is the same as {b, a}. However, we can introduce the order of these elements as a significant feature, and for two elements[8] we talk of an ordered pair $\langle a, b \rangle$. An ordered pair is simply two elements written in a particular order. For two distinct

elements a and b the ordered pairs $\langle a, b \rangle$ and $\langle b, a \rangle$ are distinct.
A particular ordered pair can be thought of as an element of a set in the following way. Suppose we have two sets A and B. By taking an element a_i from A and an element b_j from B we have an ordered pair of the form $\langle a_i, b_j \rangle$. If we have all possible pairs of this form, the set of these ordered pairs is called the *Cartesian product set* of A and B:

$$A \times B = \{\langle a, b \rangle | a \in A, b \in B\}$$

Similarly $B \times A = \{\langle b, a \rangle | b \in B, a \in B\}$, and in general, $A \times B \neq B \times A$. The Cartesian product of two sets is itself a set and is subject to all of the set theoretical operations outlined. One Cartesian product of great interest (particularly for applications in sociology) is that of a set with itself, $A \times A$.

A *relation* on a set A to a set B is any subset of $A \times B$, and generically it is denoted by R. As such it is a set of ordered pairs and we could define it by extension and list all the ordered pairs in the relation. For an intensive definition, a relationship is any property that is used to define a particular relation and the relation corresponding to it consists of those elements of $A \times B$ selected in accordance with the property. In other words, the relationship provides criteria for selecting a particular subset of $A \times B$. If $\langle a, b \rangle \in R$ for some R, an equivalent way of expressing this is $a \, R \, b$. If $<a,b> \notin R$ we write $a \, \cancel{R} \, b$.

For the set A, every subset of $A \times A$ is a relation. However, in general, our interest will be confined to only a few of these. For example, in sociometric studies the set A may abstractly represent a social group and relationships 'communicates with', 'knows' or 'likes' certain subsets of $A \times A$ will be selected. If a_1 likes a_2 then $\langle a_1, a_2 \rangle$ will be included in the relation 'likes'. Choosing A and the relationship (determining which elements belong to the corresponding relation) are empirical procedures. In sociological analyses, different relationships between variables (for example, causes, covaries with, is functional for, or determines) and differing social relations (for example, exploits, economic dependence on and controls) can be studied. Such relations are substantively different and they may also be formally different. We can define formal properties that relations may or may not possess.

REFLEXIVITY

A relation R on $A \times A$ is *reflexive* if and only if $a\,R\,a$ for every $a \in A$. If A is the set of all real numbers and R is the relation given by the relationship 'equal to' then R is reflexive. The same example basically is where A is the set of all living people in a community and R is the relation given by relation 'has the same age as'.

A relation R on $A \times A$ is *irreflexive* if and only if $a\not R a$ for every $a \in A$. If A is the set of real numbers and R is the relation given by 'strictly greater than' then R is irreflexive as no number can be greater than itself. If A is the set of living people in a society[9] and R is the relation 'son of' then R is irreflexive.

A relation R on $A \times A$ is *non-reflexive* if and only if there are at least two elements a_1, $a_2 \in A$ such that $a_1\,R\,a_1$ and $a_2\not R a_2$. Non-reflexive relations are neither reflexive nor irreflexive. It seems likely that if social relations are classified as being reflexive, irreflexive or non-reflexive, then many must go into the latter category (at least initially).[10] It may be that empirically the relation belongs elsewhere but that is an empirical problem. If A is a small group and R is 'likes' then the relation could belong to any category. However it is most likely to be a reflexive relation. On the other hand, we may wish to specify a property that a relation has. In a complex organisation, 'controls the actions of' could be taken as reflexive or irreflexive. An example in Chapter 6 takes this relation to be reflexive. Having decided this, our analysis is then restricted to cases where the relation has the property designated to it.

SYMMETRY

A relation R is *symmetric* on $A \times A$ if and only if for every ordered pair such that if $\langle a, b \rangle \in R$, $a \neq b$ then $\langle b, a \rangle$ must also belong to R. Equivalently, R is symmetric on $A \times A$ when

$\langle a, b \rangle \in R$ if and only if $\langle b, a \rangle \in R$. If A is the set of real numbers and R is given by 'equals' then R is symmetric. For the set of all males in a society the relation 'brother of' is symmetric. In early sociometric studies 'liking' and friendship were taken to be symmetric relations.

A relation R is *asymmetric* on $A \times A$ if and only if for every ordered pair $\langle a, b \rangle$ such that if $\langle a, b \rangle \in R$ then $\langle b, a \rangle \notin R$. Equivalently R is asymmetric on $A \times A$ when $\langle a, b \rangle \in R$ if and only if $\langle b, a \rangle \notin R$. If A is the set of living people in a society and R is given by 'son of' then A is asymmetric. If A is the set of real numbers and R is given by 'strictly greater than' then R is asymmetric.

A relation R is *anti-symmetric* on $A \times A$ if and only if whenever $\langle a, b \rangle \in R$ and $\langle b, a \rangle \in R$ then $b = a$. If A is the set of academic staff in a university and R is given by 'has at least as much power as' then R is anti-symmetric.[11] Note that if R had been given by 'has greater power than' then R would have been asymmetric.

Finally in this section, a relation R is *non-symmetric* on $A \times A$ if and only if there are elements $a_1, a_2, a_3, a_4 \in A$ such that (i) $\langle a_1, a_2 \rangle \in R$ and $\langle a_2, a_1 \rangle \in R$ and (ii) $\langle a_3, a_4 \rangle \in R$ and $\langle a_4, a_3 \rangle \notin R$. This is a relation that is neither symmetric nor asymmetric. For some of the early sociometric techniques and the initial formulation of the structure theorem of balance theory (Chapter 5) the relation given by likes and/or dislikes was taken to be symmetric. In general, this cannot be assumed and the relation is non-symmetric. If A is the set of living people in a society and R is given by 'brother of' then R is non-symmetric. This illustrates that a relationship, for differing sets A, gives relations with different properties according to the set A. When A could not contain any females, the relation 'brother of' was symmetric.

TRANSITIVITY

A relation R is *transitive* on $A \times A$ if and only if for every $a_1, a_2, a_3 \in A$ such that $\langle a_1, a_2 \rangle \in R$ and $\langle a_2, a_3 \rangle \in R$, $\langle a_1, a_3 \rangle \in R$.

Equivalently, if and only if, for every a_1, a_2, a_3 in A such that if $a_1 R a_2$ and $a_2 R a_3$ then $a_1 R a_3$, the relation R is transitive. If A is the set of people when R is given by 'taller than', then R is transitive. A relation R is *intransitive* on the set $A \times A$ if and only if for every $a_1, a_2, a_3 \in A$, such that $\langle a_1, a_2 \rangle \in R$ and $\langle a_2, a_3 \rangle \in R$, then $\langle a_2, a_3 \rangle \notin R$. If A is the set of people in a society and R is given by 'son of' then R is intransitive. In an attempt to construct the Mohr scale for mineral hardness in terms of scratching, substances were found such that a scratched b, b scratched c, and c scratched a. Such a triple is intransitive, but not all of the triples of substances were like this. A relation R is *non-transitive* on $A \times A$ if there are elements $a_1, a_2, a_3 \in A$ such that $\langle a_1, a_2 \rangle \in R$, $\langle a_2, a_3 \rangle \in R$ and $\langle a_1, a_3 \rangle \in R$ and there exists also elements $b_1, b_2, b_3 \in A$ such that $\langle b_1, b_2 \rangle \in R$, $\langle b_2, b_3 \rangle \in R$ and $\langle b_1, b_3 \rangle \notin R$.

In the definition of the reflexive relation, $a R a$ had to hold for every element of the set A. The symmetric relation on the other hand does not specify $a R b$ and $b R a$ for all pairs of elements belonging to A, but only for those pairs where either holds. Similarly, the property of transitivity is not defined for all triples of elements from A. Table 2.1 contains a list of certain relations and their properties.

By specifying certain combinations of these properties we obtain specific relations. For example, if a relation is reflexive, anti-symmetric and transitive it is termed a *partially ordered set*. Partial orders are used in the chapters on measurement, status and organisations. If a relation is reflexive, symmetric and transitive it is termed an *equivalence relation*. It is easily shown that if an equivalence relation is defined over a set A, then A is partitioned into disjoint subsets each one of which is an equivalence class. This relation will also be used subsequently and other specific relations will be introduced where they are needed.

Relations can also be represented as graphs or as matrices. This is left until Chapter 4 when these representations can be discussed in the context of the analysis of social structure.

Table 2.1: Social Relations and Their Properties

Set A	Relation R	Reflexivity	Symmetry	Transitivity
All people in a society S	brother of	irreflexive	non-symmetric	transitive
all males in a society; M	brother of	irreflexive	symmetric	transitive
S	as least as old as	reflexive	anti-symmetric	transitive
S	is married to	irreflexive	symmetric	intransitive*
S	son of father of	irreflexive	asymmetric	intransitive
S	ancestor of	irreflexive	asymmetric	transitive
S	has higher status than	irreflexive	asymmetric	transitive
A specific social group	likes†	non-reflexive‡	non-symmetric‡	non-transitive‡
A specific complex organisation	co-ordinates the activities of‡	reflexive	anti-symmetric	transitive

* If marriage is monogamous the conditions for this case do not apply.

† This is the most we can say in advance of studying a group.

‡ These properties can be specified in advance and our analysis would be confined to organisations with them.

2.4 Mappings

In order to discuss the process of measurement it is helpful to have the concept of a mapping at our disposal. However the only algebraic notion that is used is that of a product of mappings. Thus most of this section can be omitted in a first reading. The various notions introduced here are needed for the discussion of status (Chapter 7) but the reader can safely omit them until then.

A *mapping* (alternatively called a function) is a particular type of relation. A relation m on a set $A \times B$ is a mapping if and only if for each $a \in A$ there is exactly one element $b \in B$ such that $\langle a, b \rangle \in R$. In other words a mapping assigns to each element $a \in A$ a unique element $b \in B$. The mapping can be denoted by $m: A \to B$ or by $f: A \to B$. (The latter notation is used when the term function is employed.) The set A is known as the domain of m (or f). Not all the elements of B are necessarily used and a particular element $b \in B$ can appear in more than one ordered pair $\langle a, b \rangle \in m$. If b is an element such that $\langle a, b \rangle \in m$ then we can write $b = m(a)$ or $b = f(a)$. The set of all elements b such that $b = m(a)$ for some a in A is called the image (or range) of m. Figure 2.2 (a) and (b) illustrate some mappings (where the elements are represented by dots).

Of particular interest are the mappings, $m: A \to A$. Consider the relations 'father of' and 'son of' which appeared in Table 2.1. In terms of the properties previously discussed, these two relations cannot be differentiated as they are both irreflexive, asymmetric and intransitive. However, for each son there can be only one (biological) father, but for each father there can be more than one son; 'son of' is a mapping but 'father of' is not.

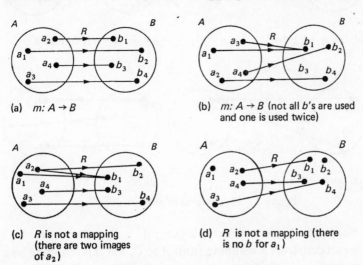

(a) $m: A \to B$

(b) $m: A \to B$ (not all b's are used and one is used twice)

(c) R is not a mapping (there are two images of a_2)

(d) R is not a mapping (there is no b for a_1)

Figure 2.2 Mappings and relations

As mappings are relations they are sets and the set theoretic operations can be used on mappings also. Mappings can be distinguished with respect to the following properties. A mapping $m: A \to B$ is called a *one-one mapping* if distinct elements of B are assigned to different elements in A. In other words, m is a one-one mapping of no two elements in A have the same image.[12] (See Figure 2.3.) Generally when $m: A \to B$ the set $m(A)$ is a subset of B and the mapping is said to α *into* B. If $m(A) = B$ the whole set B is the *image* of A for the mapping m, and m is a mapping of A *onto* B. A mapping $m: A \to B$ is a *constant* mapping if all the elements of A are mapped to the same element in B. (The image of A is a single element.) For a mapping $m: A \to A$ if $m(a) = a$ for all $a \in A$ then m is the *identity mapping* and is denoted by i_A.

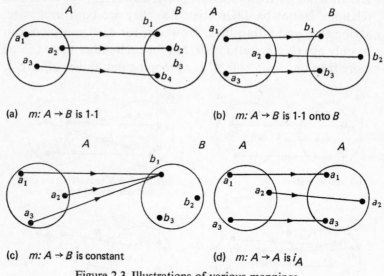

(a) $m: A \to B$ is 1-1

(b) $m: A \to B$ is 1-1 onto B

(c) $m: A \to B$ is constant

(d) $m: A \to A$ is i_A

Figure 2.3 Illustrations of various mappings

Suppose we have two mappings $m: A \to B$, and $n: m(A) \to C$. We can construct a mapping from A to C. Let this mapping be p then $p(a) = n(m(a))$ for each a, and this element is an element of C. The mapping p is the product of m and n which is denoted by (nm) or $n \, o \, m$. Here the o denotes an operation that specifies how mappings can be combined or 'multiplied'. The 'multiplication' is mapping m 'followed by' mapping n (see Figure 2.4).

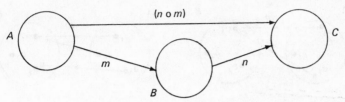

Figure 2.4 Product of mappings

Let us suppose now we have three mappings $m: A \to B$, $n: B \to C$ and $p: C \to D$ then we can construct a product of these in two ways. If we consider m and n, $(n \ o \ m)$ is a mapping from A to C and then $p \ o \ (n \ o \ m)$ is a mapping from A to D. Alternatively $(p \ o \ n)$ is a mapping from B to D and thus $(p \ o \ n) \ o \ m$ is a mapping from A to D. In fact, these two mappings are equal and the product of mappings satisfy the associative law $(p \ o \ n) \ o \ m = p \ o \ (n \ o \ m)$. We write $(p \ o \ n \ o \ m): A \to D$ (see Figure 2.5).

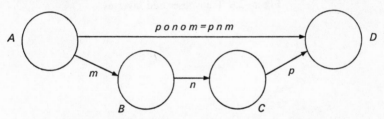

Figure 2.5 Associativity of products of mappings

Finally, let $m: A \to B$ be a mapping. This is a set of elements of the form $\langle a, b \rangle$. Suppose we construct a set of elements $\langle b, a \rangle$ one for each corresponding element of m. This set will certainly be a relation. We denote it by m^T and call it the transpose of m. It is not necessarily a mapping (see Figure 2.6). Suppose that it is a mapping $(m^T: B \to A)$ then from our products of mappings we have $m^T \ o \ m: A \to A$. If $m: A \to B$ is a mapping that is both one-one and onto B, then m^T must be a one-one mapping onto A. In this case we call m^T the inverse of m and denote it by m^{-1}. Then $(m^{-1}m) = i_A$ and $(mm^{-1}) = i_B$.

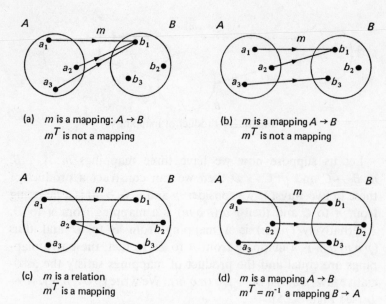

Figure 2.6 Transposes and inverses

3. Measurement

I shall focus upon some of the conceptual problems involved in measurement rather than upon particular techniques that have been designed to satisfy certain measurement requirements[1]. Measurement is simply an attempt to obtain information from what we observe. For the sociologist this information has to be relevant to the sociological problems he is studying. If, for example, he is studying the functioning of a small group he may specify in advance the sort of information he wants and then proceed to obtain this information. Alternatively, he may notice some feature of a group and recognise its relevance. In both cases the key features of measurement are information and its relevance. Both are judged by sociological criteria. However, there are different types of measurement that, in general, permit differing mathematical techniques to be used. The measurement problem is simply that of having measurement which provides relevant information and which is also amenable to sophisticated techniques of data analysis. It is a problem because the two sets of criteria are frequently held to be incompatible. In order to discuss this further, the following section introduces some analytical distinctions.

3.1 Basic Distinctions

In the opening chapter the distinction was made between theoretical and observational concepts. Suppose that O is a set of observable objects which are specified by observational concepts and further that E is a set of properties of these objects. These properties (values of variables) are also specified by observational concepts. Strictly speaking, O is not necessarily

B

restricted to a set of objects of the same type, say, a set of individuals. It can also be a set of sets of objects where we are dealing simultaneously with more than one kind of unit of analysis, for example, when individuals and roles are studied in various formal organisations. In this case, O is still a set, and we shall, in general, refer simply to the set O (although in particular instances it is necessary to indicate whether O refers to a set of objects or to a set of sets).

Let $\hat{O}$ denote the ordered[2] n-tuple $\langle O, R_1, \cdots, R_{n-1} \rangle$ where the R_i are relations defined on the set O. When O is a set of elements, each relation is a relation defined on that particular set. For example, if O is a set of individuals, R could be the relation 'knows' defined on O. However, when O is a set of sets of objects $\{O_j\}$, there are possibly additional types of relations. Each of the R_i can be a relation defined on a particular set O_j (as above when R, was defined on O). We could also have relations that are subsets of Cartesian products, $O_i \times O_j$, of particular sets[3] of objects. For example, if O_1 is a set of individuals and O_2 a set of complex organisations, the relation 'works in' would be a subset of $O_1 \times O_2$. For convenience, we shall write $\hat{O} = \langle O, R \rangle = \langle \{O_i\}, \{R_j\} \rangle$ bearing in mind that this can represent many configurations of varying complexity. $\hat{O}$ is called an observable relational structure.

In a similar fashion, we can define a mathematical relational structure $\hat{M} = \langle M, S \rangle = \langle \{M_i\}, \{S_j\} \rangle$ where M is a set of symbols (or a set of sets of symbols) and the S_j are relations defined over particular sets M_i (or Cartesian products of these sets). M can vary over a good many mathematical structures, and in particular, we are interested when M is an algebra, especially an algebra interpreted in the real numbers (see Appendix B and below).

Broadly speaking, measurement is simply a mapping from $\hat{O}$ to $\hat{M}$. However, we are not measuring objects, but properties of these objects (Torgerson (1958)). Thus, if O is a set of individuals, we are not measuring them but their properties, for example, their attitudes or their status. If O is a set of social systems, then some examples of the properties to be measured would be inequality, openess or rigidity. We therefore define $\hat{E} = \langle E, T \rangle$ as an empirical relational structure where E is a set of properties and T is a set of relations defined over the set E (with exactly the same provisos as for $\hat{O}$ and $\hat{M}$). In this case, the set E must be a set of sets of properties where each variable specifies a set of properties (values). With this distinction, measurement is properly a mapping from $\hat{E}$ to $\hat{M}$, and in general, we shall write this mapping as $m: \hat{E} \rightarrow \hat{M}$.

When a mathematical relational structure is used for measurement we shall refer to it as a *measurement structure*. It is clear that in the process of research there are mappings from O to E. This step is done quite automatically as, for each variable, we attempt to determine which value properly characterises each unit of analysis (object of O). Thus if O is a set of respondents and E_1 is the variable age, then each respondent is coded into the appropriate age category. Without doing this for each O and E_i we would be unable to determine how the variables co-vary (but for a discussion of measurement properties these mappings (from O to E) are not directly relevant).[4]

3.2 Measurement Structures

In considering measurement structures we start with the distinction between *property measurement* and *structural measurement* (Abell, 1968a). This is an analytical distinction where property measurement refers to measurement of the properties of objects. We measure properties of objects relative to each other. Using the variable of age as an example, it is clear that 'older than' is a relation between the objects of O, or preferably between the properties in E. The particular properties take on values of the variables and by so doing they have a certain relation to each other. This is not a social relation in the same way that coerces, controls, knows or likes are. If the social objects are, for example organisations or people, then each social object can be represented by an element in a mathematical relational structure and the particular relation can be represented by relations in the measurement structure. Thus these social relations can also be mapped to a measurement structure, and this type of measurement is called structural measurement. If in a particular case a property like age does define a social relation, then we must treat it as such and therefore would be dealing with structural measurement. The distinction between these two types of measurement is an analytical one and for certain variables we cannot say (independently of the empirical context) which type of measurement is appropriate.[5]

The simplest type of measurement considered by Abell is the simple nominal level, where m is simply a 1-1 mapping from $\hat{E}$ to $\hat{M}$. Each property (value of a variable for a given social object) is given a distinct label which is an element of M. It is clear that measurement at this level is always possible. However, for property measurement it is quite impracticable and further, redundant. In the case of structural measurement it is necessary, as each element has to be considered as distinct from the other elements of the structure of, for example, individuals, social classes or institutions, and our attention is focused upon the relations between these elements.

If we define a simple binary relation (see Appendix B) on a set of symbols M we can depict this as a graph (see Chapter 4). If we successively require our relations to be reflexive, symmetric, transitive or any combination of these[6] we create various subclasses of graphs. We can, by means of specifying certain axioms, define many different algebras (see Appendix B) and use these as measurement structures. The following chapters are largely taken up with the use of these measurement structures, and most of this book can be seen as an exploration of uses of structural measurement. This area is frequently described rather loosely, as the use of mathematical models. However, by taking this broader view of measurement it is clear that these mathematical models are brought within the same framework and are not then seen as an arbitrary and conceptually distinct use of mathematics.

We have seen that simple nominal measurement is redundant.

However, suppose that some properties (of different objects) are not given distinct labels but are given the same labels. This simply divides the elements of E into a set of mutually exclusive and exhaustive categories. This is called the *nominal* level of measurement.

For a given pair of elements we can say either that they belong to the same category or they do not. No further information is given by (or needed for) a nominal scale. Even so, care is necessary in constructing a nominal scale. The properties must be classified in a (sociologically) meaningful way using relevant objective and unique criteria of similarity. Clearly an investigator has to decide what will be classified, what categories will be used and also to perform the classification of items into these categories. Frequently, the categories are established by convention or by intuition, but there are available mathematical procedures which can guide this classificatory process (Sokal and Sneath (1963)). See also Ball (1965).

The mathematical structure that is usually considered next is the (strict) *ordinal* scale (but $\hat{M}$ could be less structured than this). The ordinal scale has the properties of the nominal scale together with an ordering relation. We define the order relation ($>$) such that

(i) $>$ is asymmetric and transitive,

and

(ii) $a = b$ if and only if $a \not> b$ and $b \not> a$.

The second of these conditions is stating either that $a = b$ (a belongs to the same equivalence class as b), or $b > a$ or $a > b$. The order relation is a complete order. If, for example, we consider age as a variable, then all the ages from, say 0 to 100, are completely ordered. So too are consecutive age intervals. Individuals grouped together have the same age (within the limits of the interval used) and for any two individuals not grouped together we can decide which is the older of the two. If we took religion as a variable then we could sort people into, say, the categories Protestant and Catholic, but we could not order the categories (although individual Protestants and Catholics might).

Both of these levels of measurement and, of course, all those in between, are qualitative forms of measurement. The measurement structures that we have considered thus far, are all qualitiative. Sometimes the requirement of order is taken as a minimal requirement for measurement (see Torgerson (1958), Coleman (1964)), although this rules out many measurement structures from consideration. Frequently it is felt necessary to use higher forms of measurement. Instead of knowing that a particular individual has a higher income than another we might want to know how much bigger his income is, or if unemployment is greater in one area than another, we might want to know by how much. It is clear that if we can use higher levels of measurement, namely quantitative measurement, we gain a greater flexibility in description, obtain more information about a property and possibly we can express the relation between two variables in a quantitative form.

Suppose we have measured two properties a and b on an ordinal scale and we have $a > b$. We are not able to say how much bigger a is than b and the expression $a - b$ for the distance between a and b is meaningless. Further if we also measured c and d and found that $c > d$, then with an ordinal scale it is quite impossible to compare the distance between a and b with the distance between c and d. Using four of the Registrar General's categories of social class (I, II, III and IV) we can say that $I > II > III > IV$ in the ranking of social classes. To compare the distances between social classes I and II, and between social classes III and IV is quite meaningless. If we assume the properties of an ordinal scale and add to them an assumption that there is a unit of measurement, we have an interval level scale. Given any four scale values, say a, b, c and d, the differences $a - b$ and $c - d$ are meaningful. We can decide whether or not they are equal, and if they are unequal we can decide which of the two is the greater. The scale values of an interval level scale satisfy a binary operation of addition. We have the following rules: (i) if a and b are scale values, $a + b$ is also a scale value, (ii) $a + b = b + a$ for all scale values a and b, (iii) if $a = b$ and $c = d$ then $a + c = b + d$ for scale values a, b, c and d, (iv) $(a + b) + c = a + (b + c)$ for scale values a, b and c. If in this case, M is the set of real numbers the measurement structure does *not* have all the algebraic properties of the real number system (see Appendix B). The Centigrade and Fahrenheit temperature scales are frequently cited examples of interval scales.

In an interval level scale we are unable to talk about the ratio of scale values. This is overcome if there is in addition to the properties of an interval scale a non-arbitrary zero point. It is then possible to talk about the ratio a/b for scale values a and b. The distinction between interval and ratio scales is a small one although the difference is made clearer then we consider the kinds of transformation that leave scale properties unchanged.

We can state the so-called measurement problem more generally. We have the empirical relational structure $\hat{E} = \langle E, S \rangle$ and the mathematical structure $\hat{M} = \langle M, T \rangle$, where the properties of $\hat{M}$ are dependent both on M and T.[7] Measurement can be defined as a mapping $m: \hat{E} \to \hat{M}$. Frequently the requirement that M be an isomorphism (see Chapter 1 and Appendix A) is added. However, we measure in order to obtain information about E and not solely to conform to particular rules. If we know the mathematical relations of $\hat{M}$ and other possible measurement structures, it is convenient to know their properties and the kind of manipulations that can be performed in the measurement structure. It does not follow (Adams 1965) that in $\hat{E}$ there have to be corresponding physical operations to those performed in $\hat{M}$ (or vice versa). This does not mean that as far as measurement is concerned we can do anything, but that we allow more flexibility than allowed under the restriction of m being an isomorphism from $\hat{E}$ to $\hat{M}$.

If we consider the levels of measurement as a hierarchy from the least structured to the most structured, variables measured at a particular level can also be measured at lower levels. There is no logical barrier to do this, but by measuring at a lower level we are throwing away information. For example, we can measure income using a ratio scale (with pounds sterling as units and origin zero), and also at the ordinal scale level (using the dichotomy of high income and low income). We clearly have less available information if we measure in the second fashion.

The differences between the various scales can be made a little clearer if we consider which transformations of the scales leave the scale properties unchanged. Consider Figure 3.1 which represents a measurement mapping $m: \hat{E} \to \hat{M}$. We can transform the scale that we use by means of another mapping $f: \hat{M} \to \hat{M}$, and these two mappings can be used to define $fm: \hat{E} \to \hat{M}$. If f preserves the properties of the scale used in M then fm is also a mapping between $\hat{E}$ and $\hat{M}$ with the same properties as m.

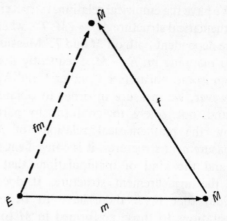

Figure 3.1

Let us consider measurement at the level of the nominal scale and suppose a, b and c are three elements of E that are mapped to (say) 10, 5 and 1 in M. Now all that matters about the elements used in $\hat{M}$ for nominal measurement is that they are distinct. Therefore, the numbers 2, 3 and 4 would do just as well. In fact, any triple of distinct elements from any set would suffice for nominal measurement. Any transformation that is a 1-1 mapping from $\hat{M}$ to $\hat{M}$ will preserve the scale properties of a nominal scale.

Suppose now we are measuring at the ordinal level and again a, b and c in E are mapped to 10, 5 and 1 in M. The order of the elements used in $\hat{M}$ must be preserved. There are 1-1 transformations that will *not* preserve order. If f maps 10, 5 and 1 (in M) to 2, 3 and 4 (in M), then fm maps a, b and c (in E) to the elements 2, 3 and 4 in M. We know that $a > b > c$ but the mapping fm is such that $f(m(a)) \not> f(m(b)) \not> f(m(c))$. The only mappings f, that will preserve the ordinal scale properties are those 1-1 mappings which preserve order.

In considering interval level scales and we again suppose that a, b and c (in E) are mapped respectively to 10, 5 and 1 (in M). In this case, not only is the ordering of the elements of $\hat{M}$ to be preserved, the ordering of their differences must be preserved also. We have $m(a) - m(c) = 10 - 1 > m(a) - m(b) = 10 - 5 > m(b) - m(c) = 5 - 1$. Suppose we consider any monotonic increasing transformation f, for example, $f(10) = 20$, $f(5) = 18$ and $f(1) = 8$, which preserves order. However, while $f(m(a)) - f(m(c)) = 20 - 8 > f(m(a)) - f(m(b)) = 20 - 18$, $f(m(a)) - f(m(b)) = 20 - 18 \not> f(m(b)) - f(m(c)) = 18 - 8$.
The ordering of the distances is not preserved as *all* orderings of distances have to be preserved.[8] The properties of the interval level scales are preserved by all linear transformations where $f(x) = ax + b$ where a and b belong to M. In our example, the three elements would be mapped by f to (respectively) $10a + b$, $5a + b$ and $a + b$. If we let $a = 2$ and $b = 3$, then they are mapped 23, 13 and 5. On examining the distances between these elements (which are the images of a, b and c under the mapping fm) the order of distances is preserved.

Finally, we consider ratio scale measurement and suppose, as before that m maps a, b and c to 10, 5 and 1. Given now that we have a ratio scale, the ratios of these numbers are significant

B*

in addition to their order and the ordering of distances between them. We have $\left.\frac{m(a)}{m(b)}\right. = 2$, $\left.\frac{m(a)}{m(c)}\right. = 10$ and $\left.\frac{m(b)}{m(c)}\right. = 5$. Suppose we reconsider the linear transformation given by $f(x) = 2x + 3$. The images of a, b and c under the mapping fm are 23, 13 and 5 (as before). However, it is clear that $\left.\frac{f(m(a))}{f(m(b))}\right. = \frac{23}{13} \neq 2$ and similarly none of the other ratios are preserved. If $b = 0$ and we consider only transformations of the form $f(x) = ax$, then the images of a, b and c under fm are now $20a$, $10a$ and a. Under such a transformation the ratios are preserved.

3.3 Measurement and Social Theory

It is abundantly clear that while sociology is replete with concepts it remains impoverished with respect to quantitative measurement. (The two may not be unconnected, as frequently theory is propounded with no concern over measurement, and scale construction has frequently been undertaken in a theoretical vacuum).

It is clear that empirical research should be informed by theory so that we can link theoretical concepts with observational concepts. Consequently, various scales are designed to measure the actual behaviour of the variable to be measured. Coleman (1964) emphasises this point in his discussion of measurement. In considering the level of a ratio scale (cardinal measurement for Coleman) he discusses two operations that need to be performed in order to set up the required measurement scale; comparison and combination (calibration). Coleman points out that it is not up to the investigator to decide, on the basis of guesses or intuition, what is to be measured. Although the properties of the various scales are important, it is imperative that scales are not constructed solely with regard to fulfilling certain measurement criteria.

(Although the subject of statistics is not discussed in this book, it is clear that what can be done statistically is dependent upon the level of measurement that is assumed. The empirical testing of a hypothesis is made in terms of observational concepts. In order that we test the hypothesis we think we are testing, we have to ensure that our data is in fact data relevant to our variables. We therefore need to have a clearly established relation between the theoretical concepts and corresponding observational concepts. The form in which hypotheses are expressed depends upon the level of measurement used, and further the statistical techniques for quantitative measures are more powerful than those available for qualitative measures.)[9]

The pressures in the direction of quantitative measures are considerable and the response to this is varied. One response is to shun all levels of measurement above that of ordinal variables on the grounds that social phenomena are not, and never will be, quantitatively measurable. While caution is warranted, such a stance loses sight of the fact that quantitative measurement is methodologically desirable. It is also adopted in the light of the kind of concepts we have at the moment; concepts like alienation, cohesion, tension, anomie, power, institutions, status, social class, and so on. This kind of concept is described by Dubin (1969) as summative, that is, expressive of more than one notion, and for the purposes of developing testable hypotheses, they are of no value (which is not to deny their value as summary concepts).

Another response to the challenge of providing quantitative measurement is to accept the concepts as they are and to guess the possible indicators of these concepts, which are then combined to give an index. However, the behaviour of this index in relation to what it purports to measure is unknown. Such indices have been subject to the kind of criticism contained in Sorokin's brilliant polemic against them (Sorokin (1956), Chapters 4–8). To the extent that they help to provide information in early inquiries their use can be justified.

There is, however, another course of action, and this is to develop new concepts. A start can be made in this direction by breaking down the summary concepts into components and discuss behaviour in terms of these components (see Lazarsfeld (1959)). In other words, this is to *act* on the assumption that summary concepts are unfruitful both in the construction of theory and in the testing of that theory. An example of this procedure is provided by Duncan (1966a). He considers the demographic variable of population/area. Now this concept is clearly defined, more so than most of the summary sociological concepts. However, Duncan considered it made up of three components; population/dwelling units, dwelling units/structure and structure/area. He then demonstrates that these components can be ordered with respect to importance, and furthermore, that one of these is negatively correlated with the other two components and with the composite variable.[10]

The need to break down our concepts into more useful ones is made abundantly clear by the renewed interest in multidimensional phenomena. In this case of status, occupation alone is not an adequate indicator and can itself be seen to be multidimensional (Cox, 1969). Currently, however, we lack the techniques to properly handle multi-dimensional phenomena. Certainly those theorists exploring this area in stratification (for example Lenski (1954), and Galtung (1966)), while throwing up many insights, do not properly cope with the methodological problems involved (Doreian and Stockman, 1969). This perhaps, is one of the really crucial methodological areas for sociology. In this respect, multi-dimensional scaling (Shepard, 1962; Kruskal, 1964a,b) and conjoint measurement (Luce and Tucey, 1964) may prove useful.

At this juncture, it would be natural to discuss the various strategies that have been used to establish quantitative measurement that is useful for sociologists. In particular, we need to look at the construction of parameters and indices and then at the way sociological hypotheses are formulated. In the following chapters we will go on to examine them in the context of structural measurement. In addition to Sorokin, Coleman (1964) has indicated how cautious we need to be in constructing indices and Galtung (1967) provides a set of operational requirements for the construction of indices and parameters. Torgerson (1958) provides an extensive review of techniques of scale construction and Green (1954) discusses this in the context of attitude measurement. A much more detailed and mathematical coverage is given by Lord and Novic (1968). These issues are discussed elsewhere (Abell, 1970).

4. Social Structure: Relations and Graphs

The word structure is used frequently in the sociological literature. Terms like social structure, class structure or economic structure slip off the tongue very easily. So easily, in fact, that it is very hard not to agree with Kroeber's caustic comment:[1] 'Structure appears to be just a yielding word that has a perfectly good meaning but suddenly becomes fashionably attractive for a decade or so . . . and during its vogue tends to be applied indiscriminately because of the pleasurable connotations of its sound. Rather than document such a statement, this chapter is concerned with providing a precise definition of structure, and exploring some of its ramifications. The precision obtained by using the following definition of structure is not bought at the expense of triviality. The model is simple and complexity can be added to it in a systematic manner. This is preferable to using the many allusions that the term social structure suggests.[2]

4.1 Structure
By structure I mean:

    (i) a finite non-empty set of elements S, and
    (ii) a finite non-empty set of social relations R.

Using this definition of structure it is immediately clear that the tools of Chapter 2 are applicable. But first we need to consider the definition a little more closely. The set S can be any set of social objects under study. If a social group is being studied then the individuals of that group can be the elements of the set S. The set R can then be any set of social relations. Frequently in sociometric studies there is only one element in R but many relations can be considered simultaneously, for example, chooses, communicates with, controls, and coerces. The actual choice of relations is an important one because the same group can have different structures according to the relations chosen. The set S could be components of a culture and R could consist of the relations of these components to one another. Alternatively S could be offices or positions in a complex organisation, or social institutions or even societies. In each case, the elements of R represent appropriate relations that are of interest to the sociologist. Such a definition of structure is clearly a sociological one which deals with social relations and is concerned with social objects as they feature in a structure.

Building upon this definition of structure the following concepts can be developed to deal with the complexity of social structure:

(i) *Structural Model:* This is an abstract formulation of a set S and a set R (as above) where neither set is interpreted. Each element of R is a relation of S to itself.[3] Thus the element R_i of R is a set of ordered pairs of elements of S. It is the structural model that is formally dealt with by means of graph theory.

(ii) *Interpreted Model:* This is a formulation of a structural model where the sets S and R are both interpreted. This means that each element of S is a particular social object and each element of R is a social relation that can hold between elements of S. In the corresponding graph these objects and relations are represented by points and lines (see below).

In order to have a description of particular structures, and analyses of such structures, we have the following definitions:

(i) *Simple Element:* This is a particular interpreted element of S. If the structure of the small group described by Whyte (1955) is represented in this way, Doc, Lefty or Big John would be interpreted elements. Similarly, examples can be given for any relevant set S.

(ii) *Simple Relation:* This is a particular interpreted element (social relation) of R.

(iii) *Multiple Element:* Such an element is obtained from S by taking a subset of S as a unit of analysis. In Whyte's example, multiple elements obtained from a group of youths would be the gangs and clubs that the individuals were identified with. Similarly, if an organisation has as simple elements the various positions in that organisation then multiple elements would be the offices or departments within which the individual positions are located.

(iv) *Compound Relation:* This is a social relation that is defined for a set of multiple elements.

These definitions allow us to move between differing types of social organisation without having to discard the framework provided by our definition of structure. Clearly by having different types of elements and relations any analysis can be made more complicated. This flexibility is desirable if the phenomena being studied are complex.

When the term social relation is used, it can refer to either simple or compound relations. The compound relations are not necessarily obtained from simple relations in the same manner as multiple elements are obtained from single elements. If they were taken as subsets of elements from R there is the danger that distinct relations are confounded. Further, the relation between social groupings is not the same as particular relations between individuals of those groupings.

The distinctions between single and multiple elements and between simple and compound relations are not distinctions that can be made consistently between empirical contexts. They are, however, distinctions that can be made within particular analyses. Frequently a theory may be concerned only with particular single elements without ever dealing with any of the multiple elements that could be constructed from them. Alternatively the single elements of one analysis, of for example complex organisations or gang warfare, would correspond to multiple elements of another analysis. Accordingly we also define:

(i) *Simple Structure:* This is the structure given by a set of single elements being mapped to itself by one simple relation.

(ii) *Multiple Simple Structure:* This is a structure where a set of single elements has at least two simple relations defined over it. It can be thought of as a set of simple structures.

(iii) *Total Simple Structure:* This is the set of simple structures and multiple simple structures for a given S.

(iv) *Compound Structure:* This is a set of multiple elements mapped into itself by a single compound relation.

(v) *Multiple Compound Structure:* This is a set of multiple elements mapped into itself by at least two compound relations.

(vi) *Total Compound Structure:* This is the set of compound and multiple compound structures for a given S. This can be thought of as a set of compound structures. Strictly, this is made up of sets of compound structures where each set of compound structures has particular sets of multiple elements.

(vii) *Total Structure:* This is the set of all structures considered for a particular set of single elements S. We could go further and take structures as elements with relations being between structures. Clearly this would provide a framework that would be extremely complex and cumbersome. It should also be a reminder that when a sociologist talks of social or economic structures, say, or of the relation between these structures, he is talking about empirically complex objects and uses complex concepts. This is, in part, why the use of an imprecise concept of structure frequently camouflages rather than clarifies the social phenomena being discussed.

The simplest of these structures is clearly the simple structure. The remainder of this chapter will be concerned primarily with simple structures, multiple simple structures, and compound structures.[4] Having begun to talk of structures there are a range of empirical and theoretical questions that can be posed, and the use of mathematics is (i) to allow us to pose these questions more precisely and (ii) to provide techniques that enable us to answer these questions.

The structure of a social collectivity (say a group) can be a crucial factor in the action of the collectivity. By engaging in social action the establishment within the collectivity of a certain structure can result. Frequently the argument is raised as to whether or not a group is 'more efficient' in its action if it has a certain structure.[5] Experimentally, this has been reduced to small task groups having to perform certain tasks with differing structures, the latter being manipulated by the experimenter (see Shaw, 1964). Organisational theorists have analysed the operation of an organisation as being dependent (in part) on its formal structure. For example, Burns and Stalker (1961) suggest that organisations with a rigid formal structure are less able to deal with a changing technology than organisations whose structure is less rigid.

Included in this type of analysis are the studies of 'leadership'. There are clearly questions as to what the personality traits of leaders are but their structural significance can be also assessed.[6] Are there congruencies between positions in a structure and the incumbents of these positions? For bureaucratic organisations Merton (1957) suggests that there are. For good or ill the structure of some collectivity does affect its operation. We need, therefore, to be able to describe this structure and significant features within it. Further, we need also to be able to compare structures. Even statements claiming that one structure is more structured than another structure require a fairly sophisticated notion of what structure is.

Do different social relations defined over a given type of group have different social structures associated with them? Again this is a question exemplified in the study of complex organisations, when the distinction is made between formal and informal relations. It is also a question that can be asked for any social grouping. If the answer to this question is yes then we need to enquire what the effect of one such structure is on the other. Are they mutually reinforcing or are they incompatible? How are such structures generated and how does a group operate with such structures? Crucial to these questions are (i) the description of structure and (ii) comparison of structures. Graph theory has been used to deal with both of these.

4.2 Structure and Graph Theory

A graph G is

(i) A set of points, $S = \{s_i\}$, and

(ii) A set of ordered pairs of points, $R = \{\langle s_i, s_j \rangle\}$. These ordered pairs are called lines or arcs. The notation $(s_i s_j)$ is more concise than that of ordered pairs and will henceforth be used. Alternatively we could have described G as the set S and a relation[7] $R: S \to S$. In terms of notation we can write $G = (S, R)$. Loosely speaking, a graph is a set of points with lines joining some pairs of these points. The similarity in the definition of a graph and a simple structure is obvious. By letting the points represent social objects and the ordered pairs a social relation we have a mathematical description of a structure. Graphs can represent either a simple or a compound structure. An s-graph is a graph with s different types of lines that may join points and these can represent multiple simple and multiple compound structures for $s \geqslant 2$. The total compound structures and total structures are best thought of as sets of graphs.

Historically, the use of graphs in sociology has developed from the sociometric study of the sociogram. The sociogram is a graph. However, the sociogram was studied visually and when S and (particularly) R were large, features of graphs became difficult, if not impossible, to discern. In the 1940s it was suggested that the information in a sociogram could be represented in a matrix and that matrix algebra would provide a superior means of analysing the sociogram.[8]

Suppose that we have N social objects represented by N points and that we number them $1, 2, \cdots, N - 1, N$. We can construct a square array of numbers with N rows and N columns. This square array is a matrix, and to indicate its dimensions, it is also called an $N \times N$ matrix. [For those who are unfamiliar with matrix algebra, a brief introduction to this topic is provided in Appendix C.] If there is a line from the point i to the point j, then the (i, j) element (the entry in the ith row and j^{th} column) is 1. If there is no line from i to j, then the (i, j) element is 0.

We now have three means of representing a (social) relation; as a set, as a graph and as a matrix. They each convey the same information (see Figure 4.1).

$$S = \{a, b, c, d, e\}$$
$$R = \{(ab), (bc), (cd), (de), (ea), (bd), (be)\}$$

(a) *as a set*

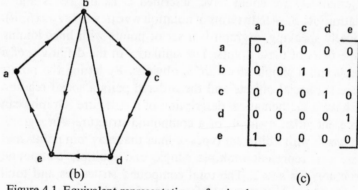

(b)   (c)

Figure 4.1 Equivalent representations of a simple structure (a) as a set (b) as a graph (c) as a matrix

The matrix for a structure is called the adjacency or structure matrix (if the (i, j) element is 1, then j is adjacent to i and i is adjacent from j) and in the analysis of a small group it is frequently called the group matrix.

Some of the basic definitions of graph theory are the following:

(i) *Arcs and Edges:* An arc is a line between two points where the direction of the line is significant. If a and b are two points then the line (*ab*) is different from the line (*ba*). An edge is a line between two points where the direction is immaterial. Both (*ab*) and (*ba*), as edges, denote the same line. Arcs and edges are also referred to as directed and undirected lines respectively.

(ii) *Directed Graphs and Undirected Graphs:* A directed graph is one where all the lines are arcs and an undirected graph is one where all the lines are edges. The latter are also referred to as edge-graphs. Figure 4.2 represents corresponding directed and undirected graphs.

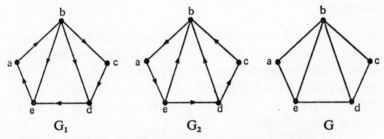

Figure 4.2 Directed and undirected graphs (a) directed graph G_1
(b) directed graph G_2 (c) undirected graph G

(iii) *Path:* A sequence of arcs of a graph such that the terminal point of each arc coincides with the initial point of the succeeding arc is called a path. The sequence of arcs (*ab*), (*bc*), (*cd*) and (*de*) form a path in figure 4.2(a) from the point *a* to the point *e*. A compact expression for this path is (*abcde*). If a path passes through a point more than once it is redundant, and if it uses an arc twice it is composite. A composite path is necessarily redundant.

A sequence of edges in an undirected graph where successive edges have a point in common is called a path in the undirected graph. If there is a path between two points in an undirected graph obtained from a direct graph by ignoring the direction of lines, and if the corresponding arcs in the directed graph do not form a path between the two points, then the sequence of arcs in the directed graph form a semi-path.[9] For example, in

Figure 4.2(b) the arcs (*db*) and (*eb*) do not form a path from *d* to *e*, but they do form a semi-path.

(iv) *Cycle:* A path whose initial and terminal points are the same (and no other point is used twice in the path) is called a cycle. The path (*abcdea*) in Figure 4.2(a) is a cycle. This cycle is made up of five arcs and, as such, it is called a 5-cycle. In general, an *n*-cycle is made up of *n* arcs (or edges in an undirected graph). If we talk of semi-paths rather than paths then we are dealing with *semi-cycles*. The length of a path is the number of arcs (or edges) in that path. An *n*-cycle clearly has length *n*.

(v) *Subgraph:* A subgraph of a graph is obtained by removing a subset of points and every arc (edge) incident to and from them. In formal terms let $G = (S, R)$ and $G_1 = (S_1, R_1)$ be two graphs. Then G_1 is a subgraph of G if $S_1 \subset S$ and for $s \in S_1$, $R_1(s) = R(s) \cap S_1$. The relation R_1 is simply R restricted to S_1 (see Figure 4.3(a)).

(vi) *Partial Graph:* A partial graph of a graph is obtained by removing arcs (or edges) from the graph. Formally, $G_1 = (S_1, R_1)$ is a partial graph of G if $S = S_1$ and $R_1 \subset R$ (see Figure 4.3(b)).

(vii) *Partial Subgraph:* A partial subgraph of a graph G is obtained by constructing a subgraph of G and then a partial graph of that subgraph. More formally, $G_2 = (S_2, R_2)$ is a partial subgraph of $G = (S, R)$ if $G_1 = (S_1, R_1)$ where $S_1 \subseteq S$ and R is R_1 restricted to S_1, and $S_2 = S_1$ with $R_2 \subset R_1$ (see Figure 4.3(c)).

(viii) *Connectivity:* A directed graph $G = (S, R)$ is said to be *strongly connected* if for every pair of points $a, b \in R$, a and b are mutually reachable (there is a path from a to b and a path from b to a).

A directed graph G is said to be *connected* (or *unilaterally connected*) if for every pair of points $a, b \in S$ one is reachable from the other (there is a path from *a* to *b* or there is a path from *b* to *a*, or possibly both for some pairs of points).

A directed graph *G* is said to be *weakly connected* if for every pair of points *a*, *b* ∈ *S* there is a semi-path between them (and for at least one pair of points there is not a path between them).

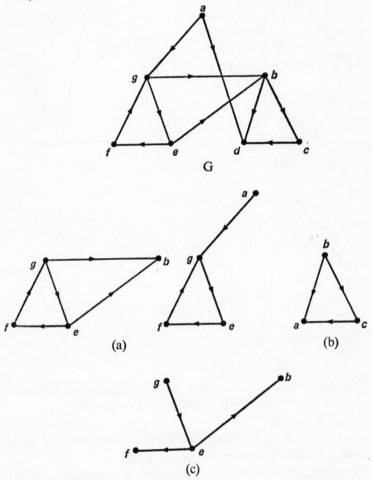

Figure 4.3 Partial and subgraphs The graph *G* (a) A subgraph of *G* (b) A partial graph of *G* (c) A partial subgraph of *G*

A graph is said to be *disconnected* if it is not weakly connected.
It is easily proved that a strongly connected graph is a
connected graph (but not vice versa) and a connected graph is a
weakly connected graph (but not vice versa). For undirected

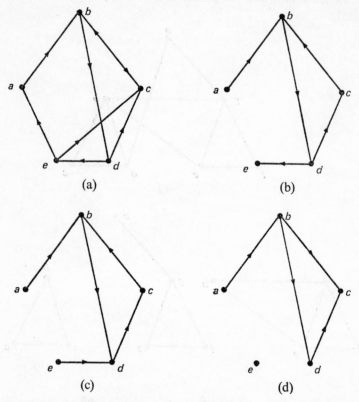

Figure 4.4 Types of connectedness (a) Strongly connected (b) Connected (c) Weakly connected (d) Disconnected

graphs the first three categories collapse into one and such
graphs are either connected or disconnected.

If a subgraph of a graph *G* is strongly connected (as a graph)
and is not properly contained in another subgraph with the
same property, it is called a strongly connected component of

G. Thus in Figure 4.5 the elements {*a, b, c, d*} and the relations between these points form a strongly connected component of the graph *G*.

We can discriminate between graphs with respect to various properties. The type of connectedness that a graph has is one such property and we can classify all graphs into four cate-

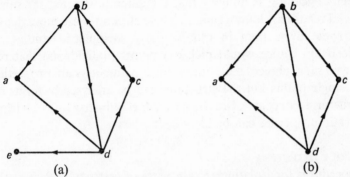

(a)   (b)

Figure 4.5 A graph and a strongly connected component (a) The graph *G* (b) A strongly connected component of *G*

gories; strongly connected, connected, weakly connected, and disconnected. This is admittedly a crude classification, but even this is of value in locating particular points of structural importance (Ross and Harary, 1959).

Distinctions can be made between graphs in terms of the properties of the relation used to define them. These properties were outlined in Chapter 2. Among these types of graph we have symmetric graphs, transitive graphs and reflexive graphs. In general, the graphs that will be considered here are irreflexive, non-symmetric and non-transitive graphs. To this list of graphs we can add complete graphs (and complete relations). A graph is complete if for all pairs *a, b* ∈ *S*, if (*a, b*) ∉ *R* then (*b, a*) ∈ *R*. This means that for each pair of points there is a line between them in at least one direction. Finally, a graph is symmetrically complete[10] if (*a, b*) ∈ *R* and (*b, a*) ∈ *R* for all pairs *a, b* ∈ *S*.

The use of graphs in sociological analysis has been concerned mainly with determining patterns and structural variation within particular graphs and with developing measures of overall variation within particular graphs and with developing measures of overall structure. We consider each in turn.

4.3 Structural Variation

Sociologically it is unlikely that the graph abstracted for some social relation is homogeneous. These structures are more dense in some parts than in others. Early sociometric studies of friendship choice would pick out points (individuals) that received more choices than others. Such parameters are properties of single points but the structures can be analysed in terms of structural concepts also. In particular, sub-structures sharing certain properties can be identified.

CLIQUE DETECTION

Procedures for isolating certain parts of a structure frequently are made easier by means of matrix algebra. Forsyth and Katz (1946) suggested a procedure whereby rows and columns of the 'sociomatrix' could be simultaneously interchanged, to yield a new matrix that reveals structural variations. (Mathematically this procedure of interchanging rows and columns is one of pre-multiplying and post-multiplying the group matrix by particular permutation matrices (see Appendix C).) In their sociomatrix, Forsyth and Katz used entries of $+$ (positive choice), $-$ (negative choice, o (indifference) and x (for self-choice).[11] The rows and columns were interchanged until there were blocks of $+$'s along the main diagonal. The proportion of $-$'s between the blocks indicated the extent of (mutual) rejection, with blocks having the greatest mutual rejection appearing at opposite ends of the diagonal. Each block represented a subgroup of individuals. Apart from the features of these blocks that have been described, it is difficult to say more about their composition. The definition of these blocks is imprecise and their membership somewhat arbitrary.

The paper of Forsyth and Katz was a pioneering one and

two research traditions (which subsequently have fused) can be traced in part from it. One considered matrices with entries of $+1, 0$ and -1 (which correspond to signed graphs) and leads on to the theory of structural balance (see Chapter 5) while the other dealt only with matrices having entries of 1 and 0. We pursue the latter here. Simultaneous row and column interchange is a fairly crude technique that has been improved upon. However, there is a bifurcation here also.

One branch uses computers to form faster and more efficient clusterings of points in the graph. Beum and Brundage (1950) provided a method of analysis that surpassed that of Forsyth and Katz. Subsequently Coleman and MacRae (1960) provided a routine which again leads to clusterings or blocks about the main diagonal that were taken to be cliques. However, this process led to non-cliqual points being superimposed upon the blocks about the main diagonal. This defect was overcome by Spilerman (1964). These techniques are especially useful for very large sociograms.

The other branch of determining clusters of individuals in a structure deals more with microstructure and uses matrix algebra. One structural feature that can be determined in this way is the clique–structure. But what is a clique? Everyday connotations of the term make it fairly obvious what is meant. However, we need a definition that is more precise than this and one applicable to all structures. The following are some of the definitions that have been used:

(i) A clique is a maximal subset of points each in a reciprocal relation with the others.

(ii) A clique is a subset of points 'amost all' of which are reciprocal relations with other points in the clique.

(iii) A clique is a subset of points such that each pair of points in this subset are mutually reachable.

(iv) A clique is a subset of points, such that for each pair of points in the subset, one is reachable from the other (but not vice versa for at least one pair of points in the subset).

(v) A clique is a subset of points as defined in (iv) with the modification that the necessary paths may involve points outside the clique.

(vi) A clique is, for a particular value of n, those points that are mutually reachable by m-paths where $m \leqslant n$.

Although six definitions have been listed (and there are more) this is not the conceptual nightmare usually created by sociologists. The second definition[12] apart, these definitions are precise, although they lead to the detection of different subsets of elements as cliques. The first definition imposes the strictest conditions as to what points form a clique. The remaining definitions all attempt to relax these restraints and allow more loosely structured subgroups to be defined as cliques.

I shall adopt the first definition and define a clique as a maximal subset of points all in reciprocal relation to each other. In locating cliques we can eliminate all unreciprocated lines. If the group matrix is G, this amounts to constructing the matrix S, for symmetric lines of G. This can be done by inspection of the entries of G or by use of the identity $S = G \times G'$ (where $\times$ denotes elementwise multiplication of matrices, see Appendix C).

A point is an uncliqual point if it belongs to one and only one clique and it is a multicliqual point if it belongs to more than one clique. Two points are co-cliqual if they belong jointly to at least one clique. By ordinary matrix multiplication we can

obtain S^2. Let $S^2 = \left[s_{ij}^{(2)} \right]$ where $s_{ij}^{(2)} = \sum\limits_{k=1}^{N} s_{ik} s_{kj}$ (and N is the

size of the structure). If k is a point in the structure and there is a line (symmetric) between i and k, and a line between k and j, then $s_{ik}s_{kj} = 1$. Otherwise, $s_{ik}s_{kj} = 0$. Clearly the matrix S^2 gives for every pair of points the number of two-step paths between them. In general S^n gives the number of symmetric n-step paths between every pair of points and (G^n the number of n-step paths between pairs of points).

If three points say i, j and k belong to a clique, then for the two points i and j there must be a two-step path from i to j (via k) and also a direct (or 1-step) line from i to j. If the (i,j) entry of S^2 is zero then i and j cannot be cocliqual, and if s_{ij} is zero then again i and j cannot be cocliqual. Consider then the matrix $S^2 \times S$ where the (i,j) element is $s_{ij}^{(2)} . s_{ij}$. Clearly if i and j are cocliqual then $s_{ij} . s_{ij}^{(2)} \neq 0$.

Alternatively, we can look at the matrix S^3 which gives for each pair of points the number of three-step paths between them. For the ith point, the (i, i) entry in S^3 gives the number of three cycles involving that point. Clearly a point can belong to a clique if and only if $s_{ii}^{(3)} \neq 0$. In fact it is easily shown that the row sum of $S^2 \times S$ equals the corresponding element in the main diagonal of S^3 for each point i. We can eliminate all non-cliqual points by eliminating those points with zero row sums in $S^2 \times S$. Let the matrix formed by removing non-cliqual elements from S be C. All the points included in C are in at least one clique.

Suppose the point i is uncliqual and that there are m other points in that clique. What is the value of $S_{ii}^{(3)}$? This is the number of 3-cycles on i and can only be $m(m-1)$. The converse is also true and we have the result that if the ith element is cocliqual with n_i other points, then it is unicliqual if and only if $s_{ii}^{(3)} = \sum_j^N s_{ij}^{(2)} s_{ij} = n_i(n_i - 1)$. This result is the basis of the algorithm for clique detection provided by Harary and Ross (1957). Appendix D contains a step by step version of this algorithm together with an illustrative example.

In the illustrative example the restrictiveness of the definition of a clique that has been adopted in this book is demonstrated. However, by considering graphs where the lines do not represent all or nothing relations but relations of varying intensity this can largely be overcome.

In all of the sociological examples mentioned at the beginning of this chapter a higher level of measurement can be taken as being more appropriate in a study of structure. There is a need for having measurement of the intensity of lines, and graphs where there are valuations on the lines.[13] Such graphs have not been studied extensively and study of them is one of the current research problems in this area.

Two approaches to the study of valued graphs have been made in the context of clique detection. In one (Doreian, 1969a) an ordinal level of measurement is employed and in the other (Hubbell, 1965) a ratio scale. A valued graph V can be defined as

(i) a set of points, S,

(ii) a relation $\theta : S \to S$ (or a set R of pairs of points), and

(iii) a relation $\psi : D \to R$, where D is a set of values.

(ψ simply assigns a value to each line in the graph.)[14]

If we have valued graphs where the level of measurement is ordinal, then the values on the arcs can be represented by integers.[15] For each successive integer we have a higher level of the valuations. For each level n of the valuations a new non-valued graph V_n can be constructed:

(i) If an arc in V has a value greater than or equal to n the corresponding arc in V_n has a value 1.

(ii) If an arc in V has a value less than n then the corresponding arc in V_n has a value 0.

This construction can be used for each level n and so a series of non-valued graphs can be obtained.[16] For clique detection, the algorithm of Harary and Ross can be applied to each graph V_n. At the lowest level the cliques will tend to be large. As successive levels are considered, lines drop out of the structure. Individual points will drop out of cliques and cliques will also tend to break up into smaller cliques. This structural variation where cliques have an inner-core, less central, and also peripheral, members can be determined simply because there is more information in the valued graph than in the corresponding non-valued graph. An example of the procedure which provides a contour model of the clique-structure can be found in Doreian (1969a).

The work in Hubbell (1965) discusses graphs where, in addition to the arcs having values on them, the points have values also. The group matrix[17] is $G' = [g_{ji}]$, and the following analysis uses $G = [g_{ij}]$. Here g_{ij} is the value on the arc from j to i. Let the values on the points be denoted by e_i $(i = 1, 2, \ldots, N)$ which are regarded as the status each individual brings to the group. These are used to generate status scores s_i $(1 = 1, 1, 2, \ldots, N)$ which are made up of two components (a) the exogenous scores e_i and (b) scores derived from the structure. The scores derived from the structure are designed to represent the value added to the status of a point by considering the strength of arcs incident to that point and the values on the points directing these lines. We

obtain $s_i = e_i + \sum v_{ij}$ where $v_{ij} = g_{ij} \cdot s_j$ is the value added to

i's status by the line from j to i.

There will be a status score for each point i and the set of equations can be expressed as a matrix equation $S = E + GS$ where E is the diagonal matrix with entries e_i in the main diagonal. We need to compute the status scores from this equation which can be written in the equivalent form $S = (I - G)^{-1}E$. Now $(I - G)^{-1}$ can be expressed as $I + G + G^2 + \cdots$ and if we denote this sum of matrices by L, the status scores are given by $S = LE$. We can obtain a solution to this equation if the sum of matrices is convergent[18] and the elements are restricted to the range $0 \leqslant |g_{ij}| \leqslant 1$[19] (which allows negative values from g_{ij} to be included).

The above use of G suggests how the structure of the group enters into the way it functions. G can also be used to determine structural variation within the group. Consider the matrix L. Each element of the matrix can be expressed in the form $l_{ij} = \delta_{ij} + g_{ij} + g_{ij}^{(2)} + g_{ij}^{(3)} + \cdots$ where δ_{ij} is the Kronecker delta.[20] Each $g_{ij}^{(m)}$ represents the strength of j's influence upon i through m-step paths from j to i. The measure of closeness between two points that Hubbell suggests is C_{ij} where $C_{ij} = \min(l_{ij} \cdot e_j, l_{ji} \cdot e_i) = C_{ji}$ where l_{ij} represents the influence of j on i through all paths from j to i. The value C_{ij} is used to distinguish between strong bonds and weak bonds. If $C_{ij} \geqslant K$ for arbitrary K the bond is a strong one and it is weak bond otherwise.[21] By taking different values of K, strong bonds for each K can be found, and the points connected together by strong bonds form cliques. As was the case in the previous clique detection procedure, cliques within cliques can be found. In Hubbell's approach the cliques found for any given K are mutually exclusive and the definition of clique differs also. (For full details see Hubbell, 1965.) The utility of this approach stems from the way it is possible to study the way the structure operates rather than just provide a description of the structure.

DETERMINATION OF OTHER STRUCTURAL CHARACTERISTICS

The matrix G^n gives all n-step paths between each pair of points. However every redundant path is included in these totals and redundant paths can be misleading according to the problem being studied. Redundancy is likely to characterise friendship networks. However it is unlikely that communication will go through redundant paths when non redundant paths are available in a communication network. In either case it is helpful to determine the redundant paths. Paths between two points are *not* redundant (in this sense) if there are other paths between these points. Redundant paths are those using at least one point more than once. Ross and Harary (1952) provide a method of tackling this problem by considering partitions of the length of the path into three parts: (i) the number of steps n_1 from the initial point to one occurrence of a repeated point (ii) the number of steps n_2 to the next occurrence of the repeated point and (iii) the number of steps n_3 from here to the end of the path. If we have an n-step path then $n = n_1 + n_2 + n_3$ where the following conditions are imposed: $n_1, n_3 \geqslant 0$, n_1 and n_3 cannot be simultaneously zero and $n_2 \geqslant 1$. For the 5-step path $(a\ i\ b\ c\ i\ d)$ of Figure 4.6, $n_1 = 1$, $n_2 = 3$, $n_3 = 1$.

A path can satisfy more than one partition. For example, the path $ijijk$ will satisfy the partition of 4 into $0 + 2 + 2$ if we consider i as the repeated point, and it will satisfy $1 + 2 + 1$ if we consider j as the repeated point. If a path passes through more than two points twice (or more often) it will satisfy further partitions. In counting these paths a start could be made by listing the partitions (of the number of steps in particular paths), counting the number of paths satisfying each partition and adding these together. However, this would lead us to count too many paths, as all those satisfying more than one partition would be counted more than once.

Our counting procedure could be modified by counting those paths that satisfy two partitions and subtracting this total from the previous total. The count would now be correct if there were no paths satisfying more than two partitions. If there were such paths we would find ourselves counting too few paths. Another modification would then be to count those paths that satisfy three partitions and add these to the total obtained in the previous step. Again if there were no paths satisfying four or more partitions this total would be correct. This adding and subtracting procedure would continue until we reached the highest number of partitions satisfied simultaneously by one or more paths. Suppose we had a particular (redundant) path from i to j that satisfied four partitions, in counting the redundant paths from i to j we would want to count this path once, and once only. If we counted the paths satisfying each partition and added them together this particular path would be counted four times. If we then subtracted the paths satisfying two partitions then the path in question could be subtracted six times as it would satisfy six pairs of partitions. Our count would now be minus two (for this path). The path would satisfy four trios of partitions and our running total would now be two. Finally the path would satisfy one quartet of partitions and subtracting it once, our total would now be one. In other words our procedure would lead us to counting the path once. This would be true for each path and for all points i and j. Thus if $R^{(k)}$ is the matrix of

c

redundant paths satisfying k partitions simultaneously then the matrix of redundancies[22] is

$$R = \sum_{k=1}^{n} (-1)^{k+1} R^{(k)} = R^{(1)} - R^{(2)} + R^{(3)} \cdots + (-1)^{n+1} R^{(n)}$$

The matrix equation that results is very large and cumbersome, although Cartwright and Gleason (1966) have provided a faster procedure.

In social groups, and in the corresponding structures, there are certain points that are of structural significance. In small sociograms these can often be spotted visually but for larger sociograms, and more generally for structures, they can be determined by use of matrices. One such point is the liaison point which is a point through which sub-groups that would otherwise be separated are joined. Formally the liaison point (or cut point) is a point whose removal changes a connected graph into a disconnected graph. Liaison points are a special kind of strengthening point. A strengthening point is one whose removal from the graph results in the graph belonging to a weaker connectedness category. Also a weakening point is one whose removal from a graph results in the graph belonging to a stronger connectedness category. The identification of liaison points is described by Ross and Harary (1955) and in another paper (1959) they discuss the determination (where possible) of strengthening and weakening points. (See also Harary et al., 1965.)

INDICES OF STRUCTURE

The structure of a group can be particularly important in the way the group operates. This has been studied experimentally by means of a group task where the communication structure is varied by the experimenter. Coleman (1966) suggests how the group structure of allocation of rewards affects its performance. In their study of the diffusion of a new drug in a medical community, Coleman et al. (1966) state that individual differences between doctors are not sufficient to account for the differences in behaviour over prescribing the drug. They study particular structures; joint hospital affiliation, office/clinic partnerships, advice, discussion and friendship, demonstrating differences in the structures account more adequately for the adoption rates of the doctors.[23] Basically those doctors who form an integrated group behave quite distinctly from those who form a group of more isolated doctors. Their use of structures is simply to construct the two groups of doctors and then simple differential equations are used to describe the dif-

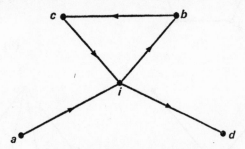

Figure 4.6 Redundant 5-step path

ferent diffusion processes within each group. (The study of diffusion processes is one that is mathematically much more sophisticated than the scope of this book, but additional discussion of the techniques is provided by Rapoport (1951) and Coleman (1964), particularly in the chapter concerned with diffusion in incomplete social structures.)

We turn now to examine some of the indices of structure. Consider the four structures in Figure 4.7 (where all lines are symmetric).

The adjacency matrix for each of these structures is easily obtained and from these matrices (or by examination of the graph for small structures) the deviation matrices are easily obtained. A deviation matrix $D = [d_{ij}]$ is a matrix where the (i, j) element d_{ij} is the number of arcs in the shortest path from i to j. For symmetric and undirected graphs the deviation matrix is symmetric, but in general it is not.

Most of the indices that have been used rely on intuitive ideas and are built from $\{g_{ij}\}$ and $\{d_{ij}\}$. If $g_{ij} = 1$ then $d_{ij} = 1$.

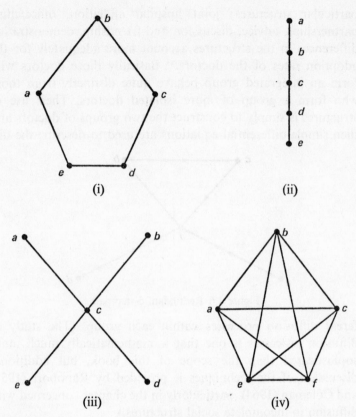

Figure 4.7 Various 5-point graphs (i) Circle (ii) Chain (iii) Star
(iv) Fully complete

$$
\begin{bmatrix}
0 & 1 & 2 & 2 & 1 \\
1 & 0 & 1 & 2 & 2 \\
2 & 1 & 0 & 1 & 2 \\
2 & 2 & 1 & 0 & 1 \\
1 & 2 & 2 & 1 & 0
\end{bmatrix}
\quad
\begin{bmatrix}
0 & 1 & 2 & 3 & 4 \\
1 & 0 & 1 & 2 & 3 \\
2 & 1 & 0 & 1 & 2 \\
3 & 2 & 1 & 0 & 1 \\
4 & 3 & 2 & 1 & 0
\end{bmatrix}
\quad
\begin{bmatrix}
0 & 2 & 1 & 2 & 2 \\
2 & 0 & 1 & 2 & 2 \\
1 & 1 & 0 & 1 & 1 \\
2 & 2 & 1 & 0 & 2 \\
2 & 2 & 1 & 2 & 0
\end{bmatrix}
\quad
\begin{bmatrix}
0 & 1 & 1 & 1 & 1 \\
1 & 0 & 1 & 1 & 1 \\
1 & 1 & 0 & 1 & 1 \\
1 & 1 & 1 & 0 & 1 \\
1 & 1 & 1 & 1 & 0
\end{bmatrix}
$$

Figure 4.8 Deviation matrices of the graphs of figure 4.7 (i) Circle
(ii) Chain (iii) Star (iv) Complete

If there is no path from i to j then the distance is conventionally
taken to be ∞. In order to preclude this we shall assume that
every pair of points have a path between them.[24] The concern
of those that consider these various structures, experimentally

or otherwise, is to provide measures of centrality for the structure (Bavelas, 1950; Beauchamp, 1964; Sabidussi, 1966). A graph is thought to be centralised if the distances are on the whole unequal. Some points are central in the graph and others are peripheral. For a finite graph the diameter of that graph is the distance between the two points farthest apart (in other words, the largest entry in the deviation matrix). The centre of a graph is made up of those points with s_i a minimum, where $s_i = \sum_j d_{ij}$.

Suppose we construct a measure of centrality that has high values for central points and low values for peripheral points. If a graph is centralised the index of centrality for a graph would be high also. If, however, there is more than one centre, the centrality index for the graph would be reduced. A graph is integrated if the distances between points are equal (and sometimes the requirement that distances are small is added). The notions of centrality and integration are clearly not independent. This does not mean we can ignore differences between them. Indeed, much of the confusion in the literature stems from failing to distinguish these differences (Høivik and Gleditsch, 1968). Table 4.1 gives some of the basic parameters that can be used (see Høivik and Gleditsch).

Table 4.1 Basic Structure Parameters

$$r_i = \sum_j g_{ij}$$

$$s_i = \sum_j d_{ij}$$

$$t_i = \sum_j \frac{1}{d_{ij}}$$

(a) *Point Centrality*

$$B = \sum_i \left(\frac{\sum_j s}{s_i} \right) = \sum_i \frac{S}{s_i}$$

$$C = \sum_i (s_i - \min s_i)$$

$$L = \sum_i (\max t_i - t_i)$$

(b) *Graph Centralisation*

$$R = \sum_i r_i$$

$$S = \sum_i s_i$$

$$T = \sum_i t_i$$

$$S' = \sum_i \frac{1}{s_i}$$

(c) *Graph Integration*

The graphs of Figure 4.7 can be compared in terms of these indices. In Table 4.2 the values of r_i and s_i are shown, and in Table 4.3 are the corresponding values of R and S. For the point i the index r_i counts the number of points adjacent to i and s_i is the sum of distances from the point i all other points.

Table 4.2: Indices of Point Centrality

Graph	Point a	b	c	d	e	Point a	b	c	d	e
(i)	2	2	2	2	2	6	6	6	6	6
(ii)	1	2	2	2	1	10	7	6	7	10
(iii)	1	1	4	1	1	7	7	4	7	7
(iv)	4	4	4	4	4	4	4	4	4	4
	(i) Values of r_i					(ii) Values of s_i				

Table 4.3: Un-normed Indices of Graph Integration

Index	Graph (i)	(ii)	(iii)	(iv)
R	10	8	8	20
S	30	40	32	20

It is clear that R and S are measuring slightly different things. The index R is counting the number of points adjacent to i, for each i, and summing the totals. As such it is really a measure of density of the graph, taking its maximum value for the complete graph and minimum value when there is only a chain of the index. S attempts to take into account the distances between points and is a better measure of integration where low values of S correspond to integrated graphs. (S takes its maximum value where there is only a chain of edges and its minimum value for the complete graph.)

Indices of graph centralisation are shown in Table 4.4. The first index of centrality B is that of Bavelas. This is the index that has been most frequently used. Flament (1963) criticises this as not really measuring centrality and Beauchamp (1965) suggests as a better alternative the index S'. As Høivik and Gleditsch point out, S' is better thought of as an index of graph integration. They suggest C as a measure of centrality, although it too fails to distinguish between the graphs (i) and (iv) of

Figure 4.7. (However, when normed (see below) C will give different values as it is normed in $C(5, 5)$ and $C(5, 10)$ for the two graphs.)

Table 4.4: Un-normed Indices of Graph Centralisation

Index	Graph			
	(i)	(ii)	(iii)	(iv)
B	25	26·1	26·4	25
C	0	10	12	0

In comparing the various indices we have compared their values for the graphs in Figure 4.7. We have only been able to do this because the graphs all have the same number of points. In order to compare graphs it is necessary to normalise the indices. This is a procedure where the effects of features like the size of a graph and the number of lines in a graph are removed from indices before indices for different graphs are compared. Normalised indices are restricted to a certain range of values regardless of which graph they apply to. The simplest procedure to normalise an index I is to determine the theoretically possible maximum and minimum values of I. Let these be M and m respectively, and the normalised index for I is $\frac{M - I}{M - n}$. Høivik and Gleditsch suggest norming within certain classes of graphs:

$G(n)$:   the class of graphs with n points.
$G(n, k)$:   the class of graphs with n points and k edges.
$C(n)$:   the class of connected graphs with c points.
$C(n, k)$:   the class of connected graphs with n points and k edges.
By imposing the condition that no d_{ij} has the value ∞ we have limited our attention to the two classes $C(n)$ and $C(n, k)$.

Another approach of obtaining measures of structure is to construct the random network that corresponds to a particular graph. A random network is one where all the lines from each point are directed entirely at random. Empirically, structures are clearly not random. Bias parameters are then built into the calculated (or expected) values of structural parameters and these are compared with the empirical network. If the biased network is a good fit with the observed structure then the bias parameters are taken as a measure of structure. This whole area requires a knowledge of probability theory and the distributions obtained are complex.[25] An application of biased networks is contained in Fararo and Sunshine (1963).

It is abundantly clear that graph theory can represent a simple structure and that the analysis of such a structure is improved by use of graph theory. See, for example, Barnes (1968) for a discussion of the use of connectivity of graphs in studying empirical networks. By means of the framework outlined at the beginning of the chapter, analysis of more complex structures can be pursued. Even at the level of simple structures it is clear that the structure itself is important in accounting for certain social phenomena. This is not to say that graph theory provides a panacea for the problem involved in the study of structure.

There are still many technical problems that require solution in this type of analysis of social structures. The analysis of valued graphs has to be pursued and similarly with graphs where the points have valuations. We also need to be able to compare structures and the various indices of structure are a beginning in this direction, although their ad hoc nature is a limitation. Perhaps one of the most important products of analysis of structure in this way is that the focus is kept on the social organisation involved.[26] This is not to ignore other features of social analysis but to assert that this type of analysis is necessary. This has consequences for the collection of data, as the prevalent method of survey analysis is not adequate to this task (see Coleman, 1958). The social organisation has to be studied and not simply the individuals within it. This chapter has dealt with various means of characterising structure without incorporating the notion of structure into a particular theory. As such it has been concerned with essentially methodological techniques. In the following chapter our concern is with constructing a particular theory with the aid of graphs.

5. Structural Balance

In 1946 Heider put forward a principle of balance to account for the organisation of the attitudes and cognitions of an individual. In the same year, Forsyth and Katz's paper suggesting the use of matrices for the analysis of social relations also appeared. The research that followed these papers was fused when Cartwright and Harary presented the theory of structural balance a decade later. Consistency theories have enjoyed a remarkable vogue and the number of studies in this field are legion. This chapter will focus on the models used by Heider (1946, 1957) and by Abelson and Rosenberg (1958) although there are other consistency theories on the market; Festinger (1957), Newcombe (1953), Osgood and Tannenbaum (1955) and others.

5.1 Balance Theory

Heider's theory was concerned with two kinds of social objects; persons and non-persons. Between these social objects there could be two types of relation and Heider was primarily concerned with the pattern of these relations. The sentiment relation (L) refers to the way a person (p) feels about either other persons (o) or an impersonal entity (x). We write pLo if p likes, admires or values o and this is clearly a positive sentiment. If p dislikes, disapproves of or rejects o, then we are dealing with a negative sentiment relation and write it as $p \sim Lo$. The unit formation relation (U) is somewhat more difficult to handle. This relation holds between two social objects if they are perceived as belonging together. Among the unit forming relations that Heider suggests are causality, ownership and similarity. When two objects do not form a unit, we write

C*

$p \sim Uo$, and generally the objects are taken as being segregated.

With these social objects and relations, Heider went on to consider a wide range of configurations of them as they appeared in dyads or triads. When considering triads, he was mainly concerned with triads made up of two persons (p and o) and a third social object that could be either a person (q) or an impersonal object (x).

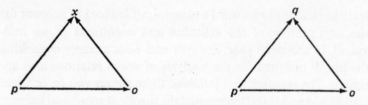

Figure 5.1 Triads of three social objects

If, in conformity with the notation in Chapter 2, we denote a general relation by R, then pRo and pRx (in Figure 5.1) are objective relations in the sense that they represent information obtainable from p about sentiment and unit forming relations involving himself. The third relation oRx is subjective in the sense that it is p's perception of that relation.[1] It is information obtained from p and not from o.

The various triads and dyads are either balanced or imbalanced. Anticipating the formalisation of his theory, dyads and triads are balanced if there are no negative lines or if an even number of negative lines are in the structure. A dyad is balanced if both relations are positive (L or U) or both are negative ($\sim L$ or $\sim U$) and it is imbalanced if one is negative and one is positive. A triad is balanced if all three relations are positive or if one relation is positive and the remaining two are negative. A triad is imbalanced if one relation is negative and the remaining two are positive. Heider treated the case of a triad with three negative relations as being ambiguous. Such caution was warranted as it makes a considerable difference whether we decide that such a triad is balanced or whether it is imbalanced (see below). Figure 5.2 shows eight configurations for a triad (*p–o–x*) with a single relation of sentiment. Clearly a similar set of configurations can be constructed if *U* is considered alone or if *L* and *U* are considered simultaneously but in various ways.

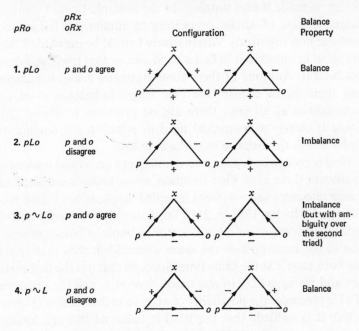

| | pRx | | |
pRo	oRx	Configuration	Balance Property
1. *pLo*	*p* and *o* agree		Balance
2. *pLo*	*p* and *o* disagree		Imbalance
3. *p* ∿ *Lo*	*p* and *o* agree		Imbalance (but with ambiguity over the second triad)
4. *p* ∿ *L*	*p* and *o* disagree		Balance

Figure 5.2 Triads of *L* and ∿ *L* relations

It is clear that both balanced and imbalanced triads occur. Heider argued that empirically, imbalanced triads were unstable and that accompanying this was a tendency for them to become balanced over time. His principle hypotheses were: (i) in a state of imbalance there are forces towards balance which will arise and at least one relation in the triad will change in order to create a balanced triad, and (ii) if change from an imbalanced situation is not possible, this situation will produce further strain.

If, for example, I (*p*) admire another person (*o*) whom I later recognise to hold a belief (*x*) which is abhorrent to me, I am involved in an unbalanced triad. This, according to Heider, is an unsatisfactory state of affairs and there will be a tendency for me to change the structure. The balance hypothesis can do no more than predict that change will occur. As to how the change is made it says nothing. In the example I could create a balanced state of affairs by ceasing to admire my friend and evaluate him negatively. Alternatively I could be persuaded that the belief in question is in fact a good one, or that my friend does not hold it. Any one of these three strategies achieves balance and there is, of course, the case where imbalance is of no consequence at all (and there are no pressures to change it). There is clearly a theoretical need to establish the conditions under which the balance hypothesis holds.

Heider recognised cases where imbalance arose and took care to discuss these also. One situation arises under conditions of scarce resources and was what he called 'implications between U relations' (Heider, 1958, p. 211). Suppose that two men (p and o) both liked some social object, x (for example, a house, promotion to the same post or the same woman) but they that could not both have x at the same time. Suppose that o is the fortunate one and we have oUx in our triad. Now pLx, and the presence of oUx precludes the possibility of pUx. In such situation (Figure 5.3(a)) it is unlikely that the triad is balanced through having pLo. Berger et al. (1962) argue that Heider's theory cannot account for this, and in fact Heider, when discussing his theory, put this case as one where the balance hypothesis does not apply. However, this case can be brought within the rubric of the balance principle. The triad is changed by removing x as it can be argued that x is not the appropriate 'social object'. What p likes (or wants) is pUx and similarly o likes oUx. If we take oUx as a social object then it is an object that p dislikes. In other words, we change the triad to the one shown in Figure 5.3(b), predict that $p \sim Lo$ gives a balanced triad and also that it is the most likely triad to occur.

Heider also placed the case of rival suitors outside the purview of balance theory. If L is taken as 'loves' then pLx and *oLx* are not likely to be accompanied by *pLo*. This case can be seen as a special case of the previous one and, as such, the same sort of reconstruction can be used. It is clear that poor definition of both social objects and social relations will result in misleading analysis. There are cases outside the scope of the balance principle that can be legitimately ignored. The triad given by *p* works with *o*, *o* plays football with *q* and *p* does not know *q* is imbalanced, but it is trivially imbalanced. Only in situations where the relations are mutually relevant (or not independent) can the balance principle be considered seriously.

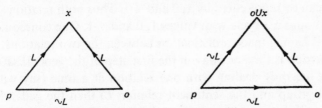

Figure 5.3 Implications between *U* relations (a) p ~ *Lo* gives imbalance (b) p ~ *Lo* achieves balance

Suppose now that we have three social objects {*p*, *o*, *x*} and that symmetric positive or negative relations hold between them. The triad can then be seen as a 3-cycle, and the 3-cycle as a graph. This is the initial step in the formalisation and generalisation of the balance principle by Cartwright and Harary. However, before we can proceed we need to clarify certain features of Heider's work. We need to distinguish between the complement of a relation and its negation. For the sentiment relation *L* (say, likes) then the negation of this is the opposite of *L*, ~*L* (dislikes). The complement of *L* is ~*L* together with indifference. For the sentiment relation we have three values; *L*, *O* and ~*L*. In terms of graph theory we can translate these as 1, 0 and −1 and we are dealing with signed graphs. These graphs are a slight extension of non-valued (0, 1) graphs. If positive relations and negative relations are considered as distinct, we have a 2-graph.

The unit forming relation *U* is a little more difficult to handle.

It is not so clear that a distinction can be made between $\sim U$ and O, or more precisely what is meant by the distinction. The complement of U for two social objects is that they are not seen as belonging together. The negation of U would mean that two objects are both perceived but explicitly regarded as not belonging together. The value 0 for U could mean either that the objects are not perceived or recognised at all, or that they are perceived but are perceived quite separately or even that one is perceived and the other is not. With these reservations we can have for the unit forming relation the values U, O, $\sim U$ and these also can be represented by 1, 0 and -1. Thus both relations can be put into a 3-cycle with values 1, 0 and -1. One consequence is that having made a distinction between the two relations, the distinction is thrown away in the first step of the generalisation. If we are only dealing with one relation at a time (say with a small group and the sentiment relation L) then the generalisation will be properly a generalisation of the psychological theory. If however, the distinction between U and L is warranted, then we do not have such a generalisation. (We could, of course, keep U and L distinct in the larger graph and deal with a multiple structure.) As graph theory can be applied to many distinct phenomena, each application needs to be examined with this point in mind.

We have a 3-cycle with possible valuations of 1, 0 and -1. If in this 3-cycle one edge has the value 0 then the cycle is vacuously balanced. However, if all the values on edges in the 3-cycle are non-zero, the 3-cycle can be said to be balanced if an even number of its edges are negative.[2] The notion of a 3-cycle can be generalised immediately to that of an n-cycle, and an n-cycle is defined as balanced if it has an even number of negative edges and imbalanced otherwise. (In such a cycle, it is assumed that no edges have value 0, which is already implicit in the definition of a cycle.) This can be expressed more concisely by use of the notion of the sign of a cycle. This is simply the algebraic product of all the signs[3] of the arcs in the cycle, where the sign of an edge is $+1$ if the edge represents a positive relation and −1 if it represents a negative relation. The sign of a cycle can be only +1 or −1; it is +1 when there are an even number of edges in the cycle and −1 otherwise. Finally we define a graph as being balanced if the sign of every cycle is positive and imbalanced if at least one of its cycles is negative.

5.2 The Structure Theorems

One of the advantages of using mathematics in social science that was mentioned in Chapter 1 is that it enables the user to prove mathematical results (that are relevant to the phenomenon from which the abstraction is made) when the corresponding result would probably not have been obtained without the use of mathematics. A case in point occurs with the structure theorem for symmetric graphs of Cartwright and Harary.

STRUCTURE THEOREM 1

A complete signed graph is balanced if and only if there is a bipartition of the point-set such that all lines within each subset are positive and all the lines between points in different subsets are negative.

A proof of the theorem (for symmetrically complete graphs) can be found in Flament (1963) and is omitted here. Figure 5.4 shows a fully complete balanced graph and its appropriate bipartition. An intuitive way to see the force of this theorem is

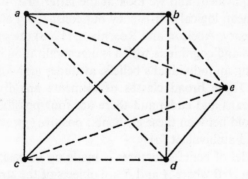

Figure 5.4 A complete balanced graph

to consider how cycles can be constructed. Suppose the point-set is bipartitioned into two subsets S_1 and S_2, in conformity with the structure theorem.

A path between two points within S_1 can either (i) never leave S_1 or (ii) leave S_1.[4] In the former case the path is clearly positive as it has only positive lines in it. In the latter case if there is a line from a point in S_1 to a point in S_2, then in order to complete the path there must be a line from some point in S_2 to a point in S_1. If there is a second line from S_1 to S_2 then again the path must have a line from S_2 to S_1 before it can be completed. For every line from S_1 to S_2 in the path there must also be a line from S_2 to S_1. In particular this is true for a cycle. Thus in a balanced graph there must be an even number of negative lines in such a cycle. Another theorem that makes the analysis of a symetrically complete graph easier to perform is the following (Flament, 1963).

THEOREM: A symmetrically complete graph is balanced if and only if all of its 3-cycles are balanced.

Having extended the concept of balance to apply to graphs on n points where $n \geqslant 3$ many different structures can be analysed using the notion of balance. There are primarily two areas where balance theory has been used (i) study of interpersonal groups and (ii) the consistency of belief structures. Formally they are equivalent and we look at the latter first. Consistency does not mean logical consistency but consistency according to balance theory. Abelson and Rosenberg (1958) present a model of attitudes and cognitions which is a generalisation of Heider's work having an individual's beliefs, attitudes and cognitions as its focus. Three broad classes of elements are distinguished (actors, means and ends) and there are four possible relations that can hold between these elements; positive (p), negative (n), null (o) and ambivalent (a).

The model of belief structures is made up of basic sentences of the form ArB where A and B are objects of the structure and r is any one of the four relations in the model. The catalogue of basic sentences can be reduced to ApB, AnB, AoB and AaB. Consider the statement: Students (A) insist (p) that all forms of closed examinations (B) are harmful (n) to the process of education (C). In terms of the model, we have $Ap(BnC)$ or ApD where D is (BnC) and represents 'all forms of closed examination are harmful to the process of education'.

A structure matrix can be formed in the same way as before. Each row and column refer to an object in the belief structure and each element in the matrix to a relation. If the (i, j) element is r it denotes $A_i r A_j$. All entries down the main diagonal are taken to be p.[5] Abelson and Rosenberg were concerned with two problems: (i) the manner in which individuals manipulated the relations in order to achieve as much consistency as possible, and (ii) how to extract information from the structure matrix. Several rules were laid down which individuals would follow in order to achieve consistency (if the model was a valid one). These rules are only operative if the individual concerned considers the elements in conjunction with each other. If a person held inconsistent (in the sense of structural balance) beliefs which were compartmentalised and never considered in the light of each other, then the model is inoperative. When we consider structural balance in social groups a similar caveat has to be made.

The rules suggested by Abelson and Rosenberg are:[6]

(i) (ApB) & $(BpC) \rightarrow (ApC)$
(ii) (ApB) & $(BnC) \rightarrow (AnC)$
(iii) (AnB) & $(BnC) \rightarrow (ApC)$
(iv) (ApC) & $(AnC) \rightarrow (AaC)$
(v) (AaB) & $(BrC) \rightarrow (AaC)$

where A, B and C are any elements of the belief structure and r represents any relation (other than the null relation). The first three of these rules are obviously designed to lead to balance and Abell (1968b) subsequently uses them as some of the axioms for an axiomatic formulation of structural balance. The fourth rule is definitional of the ambivalent relation and the fifth simply states that this relation dominates the others (the rationale for which is made clear subsequently).

Let the structure matrix be R. We want to obtain from this the permanant[7] $\|R\|$ which is defined by $\|R\| = \sum_{\Psi} \left(\prod_{i=1}^{N} r_{i\psi(i)} \right)$ where $\psi(i)$ is the integer to which i is carried by the permutation[8] ψ. $\|R\|$ is the determinant $|R|$ with all the negative signs suppressed. But first we want to know how we can 'multiply' and 'add' the relations p, n, o, a. Table 5.1 gives the necessary addition and multiplication[9] tables.

Table 5.1: Addition and Multiplication Tables

(a) *Addition*

+	p	n	o	a
p	p	a	p	a
n	a	n	n	a
o	p	n	o	a
a	a	a	a	a

(b) *Multiplication*

∘	p	n	o	a
p	p	n	o	a
n	n	p	o	a
o	o	o	o	o
a	a	a	o	a

For the addition table we can consider having 2-graphs and of combining two different arcs between two points into one. The ambivalent relation is defined as $(p + n)$ and when added to any other element, say p, $(a + p)$ remains an attempt to add positive and negative arcs together. The addition table expresses the simple procedure of deciding the net effect more than one line between two points. Similarly the multiplication table expresses a procedure for deciding the effect along a path made up of lines of differing types. The definition of the addition is not complete as we need to know what (addition) rules are satisfied. The definition of addition is completed by specifying: $r_1 + r_2 = r_2 + r_1$ and $(r_1 + r_2) + r_3 = r_1 + (r_2 + r_3)$. Similarly, the definition of the operation of multiplication is completed[10] by $r_1 . r_2 = r_2 . r_1$ and $(r_1 r_2) r_3 = r_1 (r_2 r_3)$. Finally we have the distributive rule, $r_1(r_2 + r_3) = r_1 r_2 + r_1 r_3$.

The structure matrix used by Abelson and Rosenberg has three further constraints: (i) $r_{ii} = p$ for all i (already mentioned), (ii) all $r_{ij} = p, n$ or o, and (iii) $r_{ij} = r_{ji}$. These restrictions are not severe in view of what is being studied. The first can always be changed so that $r_{ii} = 0$ or p. If there was an entry of a (ambivalence) in the structure, the structure would necessarily be imbalanced, and there would be no need to go further to establish whether or not there was balance. Finally, with the third constraint, the structure matrix as defined in this context is necessarily symmetric. In general (for example, in social groups) this constraint can also be dropped.

The only values that the permanant can take are p and a (this follows immediately from the definition of multiplication (Table 5.1(b) and the associative rule of addition). If we define balance as contained in the rules outlined above, then R is balanced if and only if $\|R\| = p$ and R is imbalanced if and only if $\|R\| = a$. This means that Cartwright and Harary's definition of balance and that of Abelson and Rosenberg are equivalent. Each product of N elements from the structure matrix simultaneously involves one element from each column and one from each row. Thus each product in the permanant corresponds to an N-cycle or a string of n_i-cycles[11] such that $\sum n_i = N$. It follows that a structure is balanced in terms of the structure matrix $R(\|R\| = p)$ if and only if the corresponding graph G is balanced. This is clearly true when there are o's in the structure, because any cycle involving an o in Abelson and Rosenberg's terms is not a cycle (for Cartwright and Harary) as an edge is missing. Neither contributes to the balance or imbalance of their respective structures. Finally the condition of symmetry imposed on R can be dropped and again the two approaches will be equivalent.

The theory of structural balance is formally equivalent to Abelson and Rosenberg's 'psycho-logic'. This is a mathematical property and techniques of one approach can be applied to the other. The set of beliefs can therefore be partitioned according to the structure theorem and balance in a social group can be determined by use of the permanant. However, it does *not* follow that because the formal structures are the same that the sociological and psychological assumptions underlying the two models are the same. The same formal analyses can be applied to the same abstract structures (which is very useful) without having to change the assumptions between the contexts. Having abstracted the structure it can be analysed without regard of the empirical context until we move back to that context and translate the results of the abstract analysis.

We consider again the structure theorem. By relaxing the assumption of symmetry and allowing the presence of zero entries, the structure theorem is easily proved for non-symmetric incomplete graphs.

STRUCTURE THEOREM 2

An incomplete graph is balanced if and only if there is a bipartition of the point set such that intra-subset arcs are positive and inter-subset arcs are negative. As immediate corollaries, we have:

COROLLARY 1: An incomplete graph with k components is balanced if and only if there are 2^{k-1} bipartitions are the point set such that intra-subset arcs are positive and inter-subset arcs are negative.

COROLLARY 2: Structure theorem 1.

This second structure theorem can be proved directly (Abell, 1968b) and it can also be proved in the 'psycho-logic' model.

One of the many formulations of equivalent properties of balance is that all the paths between two points have the same sign. This too can be used to define balance. At first sight there is a class of graphs that are balanced in the sense of the structure theorem, but for which there is no definition of balance in terms of cycles. Such graphs are the acyclic graphs. For acyclic graphs that have sequences, the structure theorem for edge graphs can be used. According to the structure theorem, the graph in Figure 5.5 is a balanced one.

There are no cycles. Clearly the conditions for the structure theorem can be stated so as to rule out acyclic graphs. This would not be a great constraint with respect to trees as it is easily proved that all trees are balanced according to the second structure theorem. For acyclic graphs in general, the suggestion of using semi-cycles rather than cycles is important. There are graphs with few cycles but many semi-cycles. In such cases, the structure theorem for edge graphs can be used.

Figure 5.5 A balanced tree

We return now to consider the case where a triad has three negative arcs. Following the suggestions of Simmel (1950) such a group has been treated as an unstable one as there is always the tendency for an alliance of two of the triad to form against the third. Each member of the triad fears the situation where he is the odd one out, and should an alliance form he wants to be in that alliance rather than be opposed to it.[12] Perhaps these arguments, together with the assumption that imbalanced states are unstable, lead to the triads with three negative arcs being treated as imbalanced. Suppose, however, that we take such a triad as being balanced, but first let us consider the implications of the first and second structure theorems.

For strongly connected graphs[13] the structure theorem leads to the conclusion that balanced graphs can be bipartitioned into two mutually hostile groups. However, in many conflict situations, multiple groupings form. Why should balance theory predict that two, and no more, groupings form under conditions of balance? (The second structure theorem for disconnected graphs could allow more than two such groupings to form but these are only pair-wise antagonistic.) This question is not unrelated to that raised in the previous paragraph.

Let us define the all negative triad as being balanced (Davis, 1967) and call balance (in this case) 'clustering' in order to distinguish between the two forms of balance. The concept of clustering is properly a generalisation of balance as all balanced triads are clusterable but not all clustered triads are balanced. Proceeding in the same way as for balanced graphs, an *n*-cycle is clusterable if there are no negative lines, or at least two negative lines, in the cycle. A graph is clusterable if all of its cycles are clusterable. A structure theorem can be proved for these graphs (Davis, 1967):

Table 5.2: Balance and Clustering

	Triad (distribution of lines)			
	3 + ve 0 + ve	2 + ve 1 + ve	1 + ve 2 − ve	0 + ve 3 − ve
Balanced	yes	no	yes	no
Clustered	yes	no	yes	yes

STRUCTURE THEOREM 3

A signed graph is clusterable if and only if the point set can be partitioned into at least two subsets such that all intra-subset lines are positive and all inter-subset lines are negative. In a set of subsets found according to the third structure theorem, each subset is called a plus-set. The partition is not necessarily

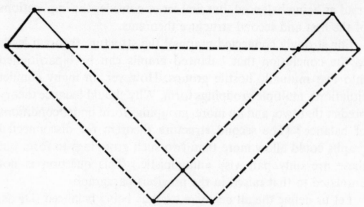

Figure 5.6 A uniquely clusterable graph

unique, but where it is, the subsets are called clusters. Figure 5.6 shows a clusterable graph with unique clusters.

With the distinction between balance and clustering, the discussion of tendencies towards balance is amplified. Harary (1959a) suggested three empirical tendencies for signed graphs:

(i) imbalanced graphs tend towards balance.
(ii) graphs tend towards completeness.
(iii) graphs tend towards positivity.

Given enough time, if all these processes are completed, the end result is a graph with positive lines between all pairs of points. However, structures seldom reach this position, and the three tendencies cannot act independently of each other. In a particular graph, balance can be achieved by eliminating a line, which is not what would be predicted by the completeness hypothesis, and balance can also be achieved by changing a positive line to one that is negative, which is not what would be predicted by the positivity hypothesis. It may be that some of the hypotheses are wrong. A considerable amount of experimental evidence[14] (some of which is considered below) is in support of the balance hypothesis, while the evidence relating to the other hypotheses is negative or inconclusive.

For certain structures (those with all negative triads) the balance hypothesis and the clustering hypothesis will not be compatible. If clusterable graphs are stable, then clusterable graphs which are imbalanced (see Figure 5.6) will be predicted as being unstable by the balancing hypothesis and stable by the clustering hypothesis. It may be that clusterable graphs are unstable, and that imbalanced structures move to balance via a clustering. Such considerations lead immediately to problems of coalition formation, and should serve also to prevent a too ready assumption that balance and polarisation are the same.

5.3 Measures of Balance

So far we have talked of graphs being either balanced or imbalanced. If a graph has one imbalanced cycle it is imbalanced, as is a graph with more than one imbalanced cycle. There are perhaps grounds for saying that the second graph is more imbalanced than the first. This observation led Cartwright and Harary to suggest $\beta(n)$ as a measure of balance where $\beta(n) =$

$$\sum_{i=1}^{n} |C_i^+| / \sum_{i=1}^{n} |C_i|.$$ This is simply the ratio of the number of balanced cycles to the total number of cycles in the graph. This measure takes into account all cycles in the graph and is 1 for balanced graphs and 0 if no cycle is balanced. For a complete graph it is sufficient to consider $\beta(3)$, the ratio of the number of balanced 3-cycles to the total number of 3-cycles, but for incomplete graphs this is not the case.

A modification to $\beta(n)$ is to weight cycles according to their length (Flament, 1963). The measure would be

$$\beta(n) = \frac{\sum_{i=1}^{n} f(i) |C_i^+|}{\sum_{i=1}^{n} f(i) |C_i|}$$

where $f(i)$ is a decreasing weighting function which decreases the importance of long cycles relative to short cycles. The major drawback with this suggestion is that there is as yet no satisfactory way of defining $f(i)$. At best it might be an ad hoc measure to deal with specific structures. Further there are no grounds for supposing it to be uniform throughout the structure. Another suggestion is that we ignore cycles of more than a given length. For some integer, say k, we can decide that all cycles of length greater than k are of no importance ($f(i) = 0$ for $i > k_m$). Instead of considering the concept of balance, we might think of a weaker form of balance, namely n-balance. A graph is n-balanced if all of its cycles of length n or less are balanced. It is easily proved that a graph is balanced if and only if it is n-balanced for all n such that $n \leqslant N$ where N is the number of points in the graph. However, the larger we make n

(or k) the more need there is for some kind of weighting function. Harary (1959) suggests a line index of balance. This is simply the smallest number of lines that need to be removed from an imbalanced graph in order to construct a balanced graph. This is the line-deletion index of balance and takes the value 0 for balanced graphs. Harary suggests another line index; the smallest number of lines that need to have their sign changed in order to construct a balanced graph. (This is also suggested by Abelson and Rosenberg, 1958). This is the line-reversal index. Harary also proves that for a given graph the two line indices have the same value. However, the line index is not necessarily a good guide in predicting which lines (if any) will change so that balance results. There was a need to consider values on the arc for unsigned graphs and the same need arises for signed graphs. If values are considered it may be that an imbalanced graph is made into a balanced graph by deletion (or change) of many weak lines rather than a single strong one.

In order that changes in a structure might be predicted, an alternative approach is to consider the various points and lines with a view to determining the strain on each of them. Local balance at a point p is given by examination of all the cycles through p. If these are all balanced, then the graph is locally balanced at the point p and if not, the graph is locally imbalanced at p.[15] A simple measure of local-balance at a point p is the ratio of the number of balanced cycles through p to the total number of cycles through p. If $|C_i^+|$ and $|C_i^-|$ denote respectively the number of balanced and imbalanced cycles through the point i, then the measure of local balance is $\beta = |C_i^+|/|C_i|$ where $|C_i| = |C_i^+| + |C_i^-|$.

Davis (1967) considers the strain on an arc due to indirect paths between the two points at the ends of the arc. Clearly the notion of structural strain caused by imbalance or non-clustering is different according to which of these is considered. For two points we have a direct line between them and indirect paths from one to the other. Given a particular n-step path from i to j, we can predict what the (i, j) line would be for a balanced cycle (sequence). Clearly the direct line 'implied' by the indirect path may or may not be compatible with the direct line that is already there, and accordingly the line is free from, or is not free from, strain. For 3-cycles we can construct[16] Tables 5.3 and 5.4. Clearly from either of these tables we can make predictions of (i) what changes of the direct line will occur, or (ii) if there is no direct line, what line will be induced. Such an analysis is clearly complicated when there is more than one indirect path between a given pair of points (which again involves assessing the relative effects of paths of differing length).

Table 5.3: Arc Strains for Balancing in 3-cycles

Direct Line	Indirect Line ++ / ++	Indirect Line +- / +-	Indirect Line -- / --
+	strengthened	strained	strengthened
O	latently positive	latently negative	latently positive
−	strained	strengthened	strained

Table 5.4: Arc Strains for Clustering in 3-cycles

Direct Line	Indirect Line ++ / ++	Indirect Line +- / +-	Indirect Line -- / --
+	strengthened	strained	strengthened
O	latently positive	latently negative	latently positive
−	strained	strengthened	strengthened

5.4 Construction of Signed Structures

The sorts of triads Heider was talking about are fairly clear, but in the subsequent generalisation of his theory this is no longer the case. The majority of work done on structural balance has been concerned with small groups and with belief systems. With the latter it is fairly clear that our data must come from the individual whose beliefs are considered. Abelson and Rosenberg were concerned with this and more recently Boalt (1969) has looked at the values of a researcher in a way that is fully in accord with clustering theory. The values that a researcher subscribes to form clusters such that values in the same cluster are positively correlated and values in distinct clusters are negatively correlated. If we wish to analyse culture with respect to balance, then we need to select the items of culture. This would involve us in the difficulties of cultural anthropology (but no more than this). Harary has emphasised that the relations in a signed structure must be inherently positive or negative, and further, the units for which the relations are considered must form a whole.

Cartwright and Harary made their generalisation primarily with small groups in mind. When we study a small group it is relevant to ask whether we need to look at objective or subjective relations. Most research has focused on objective relations where the data is collected from separate individuals about their own positive and negative perceptions and evaluations within the group. The resultant structure is constructed with information from all the individual members and the lines incident from them. The balance hypothesis is then examined for such a group. Methodologically this is not quite so easily performed. A uniform scale from a high negative relation through to a high positive relation can be made symmetric. However, there tends to be a bias against reporting negative evaluations even when they are present. Further, such a structure may not even exist. *If* structural balance is a generalisation from Heider's theory, then what should be studied is the balance properties of the group as seen by each individual. An objectively imbalanced structure (even if such a thing is meaningful) may be balanced according to the perceptions of each unit in that structure.

If we are interested in studying the objective structure there are several procedures open to us. We can assume (as part of the conditions for which our hypotheses are applicable) that perception of the group is accurate for each member. The objectively and subjectively defined structures are then the same. A slightly weaker assumption is that all the perceptions of the group are the same, and thus all the perceived structures are the same. Finally, and this has been implicit through much of this chapter, we can study the 'objective' and 'subjective' structures in relation to each other. Heider's theory was generalised mathematically, and there is no reason to assume that the tendency towards balance in belief structures is applicable to groups of individuals. However, another empirical finding, or assumption as the case may be, can be formulated; such structures tend towards balance. As it is formulated, this hypothesis does not rest on Heider's theory at all. The two may well be related but we do not have to assume this and the existence of such a relation becomes an empirical problem.

In assessing the relative merits of studying the objective and subjective structures we can only briefly consider the well conducted experiment of Taylor (1967). Taylor was concerned with sorting out which structures conform to the balance hypothesis when objective or subjective lines are in the structure. The mul-

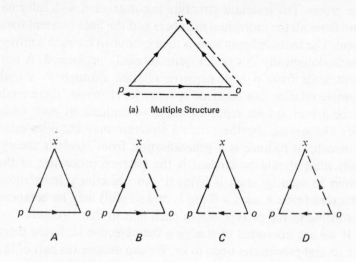

(a)   Multiple Structure

(b)   Simple Structures

Figure 5.7 Structures with objective and subjective lines
(a) Multiple structure (b) Simple structures

tiple structure of Figure 5.7 represents objective lines by solid lines and subjective lines by dashed lines. The line corresponding to (pRx) is in the sense used here, both objective and subjective and appears in all of the structures. It is possible to consider in turn each of the other triads with particular lines being objective or subjective. The structure A is composed of objective relations only, and it is this structure that can be thought of as being generalised to the graphs of Cartwright and Harary. The structure B is that considered by Heider with oRx being the relation as perceived by p.[17] Structures C and D are new structures constructed from A and B by having the pRo relation considered as oRp as perceived by p.

The procedure of the experiment is given in Taylor's article. He was able to construct triads corresponding to each simple structure in Figure 5.7(b). The format of the experiment was that of a discussion between p and o about an issue x where o played a stooge role. Each discussion was started either with a balanced or an imbalanced triad and the experimenter was able to observe changes in p's evaluation of o and changes of p's opinion concerning x as a result of the discussion. The conclusion of the experiment was that the balance hypothesis was confirmed in the A and B structures but not in the C and D structures. Clearly one experiment is insufficient, but it is an important one as it does provide support for the balance hypothesis and begins to examine structures with objective and subjective relations.

In considering structural balance it may be that it is more fruitful to consider a multiple simple structure in place of a compound structure. A case in point is the attempt to apply balance theory to international relations (Harary, 1961; Doreian, 1969b). Both studies considered relations in the Middle-East and both were limited to being *post facto* studies. While the former study considered a single structure with many relations, the latter attempted to separate different relations and with them separate structures. It was found that changes (in terms of balance) in one structure could induce changes in other structures, and that it was possible to begin to discuss the conditions under which the balance hypothesis was relevant when distinct structures were considered.

5.5 Structural Balance as a Deductive Theory

Heider attempted to make his theory more viable by establishing that it could be integrated into the more general context of organismic psychology.[18] Davis (1963) proceeds in the opposite direction, as it were, by using structural balance to provide the initial postulates for a deductive system of hypotheses. These hypotheses range over a wide range of topics and come from many separate studies. In as much as these hypotheses are accurately represented in terms of balance theory, the evidence in support of them is indirectly supporting evidence for the postulates drawn from balance theory. It is more important, however, that structural balance provides a possible explanatory principle for a wide range of sociological propositions concerning social relations.

The social relations of similarity and those of differences between people have often been used to account for human behaviour. Davis focusses primarily upon the former when he defines similarity as the correlation between individuals over a set of attributes. However, when group structure is considered the differences between people enter explicitly. The basic definitions used by Davis are those of graph theory,[19] the p–o–x triad, the sentiment relation and the unit formation relation of Heider's theory. The basic postulates are those of balance theory and Festinger's (1954) hypothesis (of social comparison) that the tendency of an individual to compare himself with another individual, diminishes as the difference between the two increases.

With these postulates Davis deduces the hypotheses relating similarity, liking and joint activity of individuals within a small group that were proposed by Homans (1950). The results concerning the cross-pressure hypothesis (Berelson et al., 1954) are derived and, more importantly, generalised. To the extent that group structure develops through the formation of cliques based on liking, hypotheses concerning this development of structure are also derived. (Here some of the hypotheses of Lipset, Trow and Coleman (1956) and Coleman (1957) on the internal differentiation of groups are featured.)

By characterising groups by the number (many, few) of dimensions relevant to group structuring and the association (high, low) between these dimensions, Davis sets up a simple four-fold table of types of group structure. Using this and the previous characterisations of structure he then derives hypotheses about the way innovations are introduced to a group, the way in which these innovations diffuse through the group and the manner in which conflict is handled by the group. Finally, there are hypotheses of relative deprivation that are (less convincingly) formalised and derived. For a full list of the deductions (fifty-six in all) the reader is referred to the article by Davis.

Structural balance can, therefore, provide a set of axioms from which a large number of sociological propositions can be derived. This does not mean, of course, that these propositions are all empirically valid. However, the deductive form in which the theory is cast makes it far easier to locate particular hypotheses and their importance than would be the case if we had simply a collection of propositions seemingly unrelated. This is especially the case if evidence is found that would lead to the rejection of a particular hypothesis.

It clearly would be a mistake to attempt to place all social theory within the rubric of structural balance. Structural balance is not a general social theory; it is no more than part of such a theory. The conditions under which balance theory is applicable need to be clearly stated[20] both with regard to testing particular hypotheses and establishing how it relates to other theoretical formulations. What is abundantly clear is that structural balance is not a trivial approach to a limited number of social phenomena. However, with this said, it is also clear that it falls short of adequacy in the face of empirical reality. One deficiency has already been touched upon, namely, the absence of clearly specified conditions under which the balance principle, as it has been called, is operative. Another deficiency is that limited tools have been used. For example, we need to create a generalisation (not only in terms of balance theory) that deals with graphs with valued arcs. Davis' work does this but only in a limited way. We need to be able to handle more complex structures and it is here that a mathematical formulation of the theory should prove useful because it is in this form that it can most easily be generalised, and it is a generalisation of structural balance that is needed. We need not stop here either. There is a large array of algebraic tools that can be potentially useful in handling notions of social structure.[21]

6. Formal Organisations

Modern society is increasingly dominated by formal organisations which can be defined as forms of social organisation that has been purposefully created in order to attain certain goals. This state of affairs has been lamented over by some social critics and welcomed by others. Social theorists have not been inactive in analysing these social phenomena and a vast and scattered literature attests to this. In an excellent summary article (Udy, 1965) there is a list of hypotheses concerning organisational phenomena. These hypotheses deal with the relation between organisation and its environment (which Udy takes to be the wider society and technology), the internal structure of the organisation, the conditions under which particular aspects of the internal structure are emphasised, organisational requirements and the changes in these as they effect the running of the organisation and the factors determining informal behaviour.

It is clear that organisational structure is an important feature of organisations, but it is equally clear that the study of formal organisations cannot be reduced to a study of organisational structure. Thus while this chapter is focused on organisational structure it does not mean that structure can be studied completely in isolation.

6.1 Organisational Structure and Graph Theory
Perhaps the most important characteristics of formal organisations are the type of power displayed and manner in which it is exercised. The majority of typologies of organisations (see, for example, Etzioni (1961a), Gouldner (1954) and Stinchcombe

D

(1967)) all attempt to make use of power in distinguishing between different organisations. The formal relation of 'has power over' can be abstracted and represented as a graph. Care has to be exercised in choosing what social relations and what social objects are represented in this manner. The points can be taken to represent roles, positions, offices, individuals or tasks. Clearly the relations that are studied are dependent upon what we abstract as points. There have been several suggestions as to how graph theory can be used in the study of formal organisation, and one of them is drawn on, in part, for the material of this section.[1]

Suppose we have a set of tasks $T = \{t_i\}$ which have to be performed, a set P of organisational positions and a set S of individuals filling these organisational positions. Given that there is a set of tasks then part of the organisational blue-print would be a specification of the inter-relation of these tasks, particularly their time ordering. This can be defined as a task procedure graph T_1. This could be abstracted into a graph with the points representing tasks and the lines representing 'is performed before'. We could also represent by a graph the relation 'fills' defined on $S \times P$ where each line is directed from some point in S to a point in P. It is important to note that it is a relation from S to P and not a mapping that is involved.[2] Similarly, we can construct a graph to represent a relation from P to T which could be 'is responsible for performing'. Finally we could have a graph defined upon the set P where the relation involved is 'has control over', and the graph represents the organisational chart.[3]

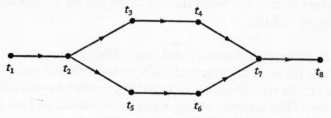

Figure 6.1 A task precedence graph

The task precedence graph T, has some use but this is fairly limited. In such a graph if two tasks are such that it does not matter which is performed first, then there will be no direct line between them. The points t_3 and t_5 (Figure 6.1) is such a pair of points, as is the pair t_3 and t_6. However, t_5 must be performed before t_6. Neither of the tasks t_7 and t_8 can be performed until all of the preceding tasks have been completed, and none of the remaining tasks can be performed until t_1 and t_2 have been performed.

Task precedence structures could be examined in terms of their complexity, and could, in part, contribute to the overall complexity of an organisation. This, however, is not so easily performed. If the completion of a set of tasks is the 'goal' of an organisation, then an intricate structure could be designed so that there are many paths from the first task to the last. Indeed, there could be more than one starting point and more than one terminal point to ensure this. If for a moment we go back to Figure 6.1, the task structure is vulnerable at the points t_1, t_2, t_7 and t_8. If any of these tasks are not performed then the organisational goal cannot be achieved. In these terms, large parts of the British car industry display this kind of vulnerability where disruption at strategic points can disrupt the whole of production. Such structures are vulnerable.[4] This kind of analysis is clearly a simplified one, although a closer look at the simplicity is worthwhile. The tasks need not be so dependent upon each other, which says no more than some structures can be made less vulnerable than others. An example is given by Stinchcombe and Harris (1969) where one operation in a steel plant on hot steel is a vulnerable point as the metal has to be worked when it is hot, whereas an operation performed on cold steel is less vulnerable as cold metal is easily stored or diverted to alternative machines. Clearly, the occupant of the positions responsible for one (or more) of these 'vulnerable' tasks can derive considerable importance from this position. The need the individual may feel to do this and the extent to which he acts on this, will probably be related to the overall structure of control of the organisation.

Not only is it possible for particular forms of control to deny him basic rights of control over his work, but the organisation can be structured to prevent the existence of such positions.

Tasks are likely to be qualitatively different and part of this difference is reflected in the extent to which tasks can be specified in this manner. One difference between particular positions is the extent to which their tasks can be included in such a graph. Clearly delineated jobs can be included in this way and this is indicative of the lack of individual freedom in performing these tasks. It is precisely those jobs that deprive the worker of any say in the place and performance of them that can be included in a task precedence graph. The further up the organisation chart the more scope for decisions and individual freedom there is for those in higher positions.

Such 'tasks' become more and more difficult to represent in a task precedence graph.

This line of analysis leads to another aspect of complexity. The greater freedom of action and range of possible activities the more complex is a particular task or set of tasks. Thus an organisation that specifies closely most of the tasks may have a complex structure in terms of the graph T, but is less complex in that fewer positions have complex tasks. This kind of variation is clearly dependent upon size, as large organisations can be complex in both senses. There is the possibility that organisations differ completely in that at one extreme most tasks are simple (with individual responsibility for them clearly delineated) and, at the other extreme, few are.

We turn now to consider the relation of control (and other relations) in more detail. Consider the hypothetical example of the small structure in Figure 6.2. In Chapter 4 it was demonstrated that if G was the adjacency matrix for a group then G^2 gave the number of two-step paths. Suppose in this case C represents the matrix corresponding to 'control' and J the matrix for the 'information' structure and S the multiple simple structure. Separating the two relations, we have $S = C + J$ (see Stinchcombe, 1961). The matrix of composite 2-paths is given by S^2 and it is clear that there can be four such paths; (i) two control lines, (ii) a control line followed by an information line, (iii) the reverse of (ii) and (iv) two information lines. In other words, $S^2 = C^2 + CJ + JC + J^2$ (and we do not necessarily have $CJ = JC$). In this simple case we are dealing only with 2-graphs and between two points there can be both types of line. As in the simple case, higher powers of S can be considered if longer paths are of interest. A third formal

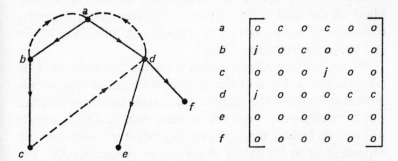

Figure 6.2 (a) Joint structure (b) Joint structure matrix S

relation, represented by K, can be included where $S = A + J + K$ and $S^2 = (A^2 + J^2 + K^2) + (AJ + JA) + (AK + KA) + (JK + KJ)$. With a complex structure (made up of more than one relation) this type of analysis becomes very cumbersome.

We have left out of consideration the informal structure which tends to be created by individuals and groups as a response to their social needs. It is not possible to indicate what informal structure will arise given a particular formal structure nor to specify the ideal combination of the formal and informal structures. There are many informal structures that could be created by using the social relations of likes, knows, communicates with, seeks advice from and so on. Each of these generates an informal social structure. We know also that there are informal leaders, and in addition to formal structures of control there are similar informal structures. It is clear that a formal organisation can be thought of as a multiple simple structure, a multiple compound structure or even a total structure, and that we cannot talk simply of 'the' structure of an organisation.

This does not mean that we solely consider the most general model. We could take one of the simple structures, say the formal control structure, and examine whether or not it constrains the others. Formal and informal structures can be compared. If for example there is a bottle-neck in the formal structure, this can be circumvented informally. Alternatively, features of the formal structure can be disrupted in the informal structures. Many of the qualitative differences between formal organisations may be due to, or can be expressed as, differences within and between certain structures.[5]

Among the hypotheses culled from the literature by Udy (1965) are several that explicitly involve structural notions: the more decentralised the authority structure, the more cohesive will be the informal relations between peers and their morale will also be higher. Both of these dependent variables are also dependent upon the extent of horizontal communication. The quality of relations between superiors and their subordinates is dependent on how much control is exercised (informally) through interaction. Not always is there a gross discrepancy between organisational goals and individual goals and, the more cohesiveness is based upon commitment to organisational goals, the less need there is for formal control as greater informal organisation will have resulted from the cohesiveness.

Most of the hypotheses listed by Udy sound plausible, and each has been 'established' by at least one piece of research. It is clear that when structural notions are considered, graph theory provides a ready means of representing them. It also becomes clear that much of the research has not been posed in these terms, and to do so could possibly distort these results. Thus while indices of centrality, integration and cohesiveness are discussed in Chapter 4, it might be claimed that this is not what was meant by the respective terms. What is abundantly clear is that notions of structure are more complex than they are usually taken to be. Can two situations with different structures be compared to see which has the most amount, or degree, of structure? If in fact they can, then we need to specify how to go about this, and if not, organisational theorists will have to be wary of using terms that can be interpreted in radically different ways.

6.2 Co-ordination and Semi-lattices[6]

For some theorists, the hallmark of social organisation is the 'need' for co-ordination. The structure of a formal organisation is one designed to maximise control (of many individuals by a few) and the central feature of the structure of a formal organisation is its hierarchical means of control over the actions of individuals. This is particularly so for formal organisations as the activities of the organisation's members must meet certain requirements and then be co-ordinated to achieve a particular objective. The work of Litterer (1963) is avowedly one to help managers in the running of their organisations, and as such, focuses on co-ordination. This emphasis is taken up by Cox (1968) in a discussion of management that provides some rationale for the use of semi-lattices as a model for forma organisations.[7]

The co-ordination of diverse activities is achieved through having a division of labour and a central source of authority The division of labour is both horizontal, which divides similar tasks among a group of workers, and vertical, which specifies who co-ordinates who. In concrete terms (and in terms of the previous section) this is a distribution of tasks to positions, where some of the tasks are the co-ordination of other positions The central source of authority has been taken as top management who provide the planning and policy decisions for the entire organisation.

On this basis, Cox (1968) has delineated a series of levels which represent fundamental steps up the hierarchy within a complex organisation. Level 1 is made up of those positions that deal directly with the organisation's output. The occupants of these positions have simply a set of tasks to perform and have no further involvement in the organisation. Certainly they have no formal authority over other workers. Level 2 is made up of those positions who are responsible for co-ordinating the activities of those at level 1. The incumbents of these positions have authority over those below them, but again they are not involved in planning or policy making. These positions are characteristically those of foreman or supervisor. The group of positions made up of a given single position together with those co-ordinated by the occupant of this position is termed a work unit.

The positions at level 3 in the hierarchy are responsible for the co-ordination of at least two work units. This can be reduced to the co-ordination of the foremen or supervisors of these work units. Cox regards these as managerial and labels this level 'middle and junior managerial'. Level 4 positions co-ordinate the level 3 positions, which will involve the delegation of work and responsibility to the lower managerial positions. This level of management is termed 'senior managerial' and can be identified as department or division heads. Finally, at level 5, we have the top management which is concerned with establishing policy and delegating authority to the senior management. Clearly these distinctions are primarily heuristic and also vary from organisation to organisation.[8] (This particular outline of an organisational hierarchy could also have been presented in terms of status but, for the moment, we are intent on providing a formal model of the co-ordination relation.)

Consider the various structures shown in Figure 6.3. They each represent an algebraic structure with different algebraic properties. The relation of inclusion between finite sets is a partial order relation and we shall use $\subseteq$ to denote this relation. Suppose we have a subset $A \subset S$. If there is an element s such that $s \supseteq a$ for every element $a \in A$, then s is called an *upper bound* of A. (Similarly if $s \subseteq a$ for each $a \in A$, then s is a *lower bound*.) For a set A we can form the set T of all upper bounds of A, and if an element s (in T) is a lower bound of T, then s is the *least upper bound* of A. (If for the set A, T is the set of all the lower bounds of A and s (in T) is an upper bound of T, then s is the *greatest lower bound* of A.) Consider the structures in Figure 6.3(a) and (b). Let $A = \{f, g\}$. In Figure 6.3(a), each of the elements a, b, c, d, e is an upper bound of A but there is no least upper bound, whereas in 6.3(b) only the elements a, c and e are upper bounds, but there is a least upper bound of A, namely e.

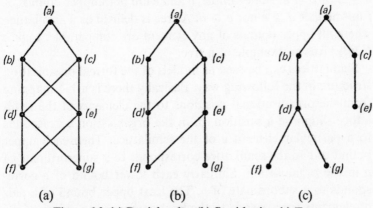

(a)   (b)   (c)

Figure 6.3 (a) Partial order (b) Semi-lattice (c) Tree

A *semilattice* can be defined as a partially ordered set in which every pair of elements has a least upper bound (see Appendix A for an alternative definition of a semilattice). We can define another semilattice as a partially ordered set in which every pair of elements has a greatest lower bound. The former is called a union-semilattice and the latter an intersection-semilattice.[9] Throughout the following we will deal only with union-semilattices, and with this understanding, we shall refer simply to semilattices. It is clear that Figure 6.3(b) is a semi-lattice.

A *maximal element* of a partially ordered set S is an element m such that $a \not\supset m$ for every $a \in S$. The greatest element of a partially ordered set is an element g such that $g \supseteq a$ for every element $a \in S$. A partially ordered set does not necessarily have a greatest element as it can have more than one maximal element. If, however, it does have a greatest element, this

D*

element is unique and it is the only maximal element. Every finite union-semilattice has a greatest element and every subset of a finite union-semilattice has a least upper bound (see Appendix A). If we consider the semilattice of Figure 6.3(b), it is clear that for particular elements, not every upper bound is comparable. Two distinct elements a and b are comparable if $a \supseteq b$ or $b \supseteq a$. For example, d and e are both upper bounds of f but neither $d \supseteq e$ nor $e \supseteq d$. A tree is defined as a semilattice where all upper bounds of any element are comparable. Figure 6.3(c) gives an example of a tree.

Semilattices can be used as models of the formal organisation structure in the following way. Basically there is a 1-1 mapping from the organisational positions to the elements of the semilattice. Suppose a position, p, in the organisation corresponds to a particular element e of the semilattice. Then each upper bound of e in the semilattice corresponds to a superordinate of p in the organisation. Similarly each lower bound of e corresponds to a subordinate of p. The least upper bound of a pair of elements corresponds to the least common supervisor of the corresponding pair of positions in the organisation. The ordering relation is that of superordination. In claiming that this relation is a partial ordering we are saying that the occupant of each position is a superordinate to himself (which is not really so bizarre, and in fact, says nothing about relations between different elements), no two individuals can simultaneously be superordinate to each other and finally the superordinate of a superordinate is also a superordinate.

Before we can say that a semilattice can, in fact, serve as a model for a formal organisational structure, we need to ensure that every pair of elements has a least upper bound or, in terms of the organisational structure, that each pair of positions has a least common superordinate position. In fact we do not do this, which leads us to the basic distinction between the approach in this section and the approach in the previous section. These graphs were being used to *describe* particular structures while here we are *conjecturing* that semilattices will provide an adequate description of the formal organisation under certain conditions.

Certainly we can claim that formal authority structures in formal organisations tend to be trees. We can then examine the conditions under which trees would be predicted. If in constructing an organisation the organisational elite was concerned to minimise conflicting orders, then a tree structure would serve this purpose. Every member of the organisation (except the head of the organisation) would have one and only one superordinate. There would be no possibility of conflicting orders as each individual has only one source from which orders could be received.

It is clear that while the tree structure solves the problem of minimising conflicting orders, it does so at the expense of being a vulnerable structure. Thus at every line, a tree is vulnerable. Any failure to give orders to a subordinate would be disruptive, and in the structure of the organisation there may be an attempt to protect the organisation from this. Passing orders along a chain of positions may be wasteful or inefficient as well.

However, the role of a superordinate may involve more than simply giving orders. A distinction can clearly be made between providing information to subordinates and encouraging motivation. The latter becomes important if we recognise that individuals do not respond solely to economic factors. To the extent that motivation (to participate) is dependent upon an individual's peers and subordinates as well as his superordinates, the importance of adhering to a tree structure throughout the whole structure is lessened. The reception of information from multiple sources is also less difficult to deal with than receiving orders from more than one source. Further, the more knowledge and expertise an individual has, the less difficulty he experiences with conflicting information.[10] Arguments of this nature (if only for the positions where the incumbents are allowed to take decisions and have powers of discretion) lead to a reduction of emphasis upon the need to avoid conflicting orders. It follows that in some cases violation of the tree structure can become desirable, or at least not undesirable.

The use of a tree as a model of organisational structure becomes overly restrictive. But trees are no more than special cases of semilattices, and in looking for a less restrictive structure than a tree, we can consider the semilattice and focus instead upon the co-ordination relation. The rationale for this approach is provided in the previous discussion of the work of Litterer and of Cox. Let $c = C(S)$ denote the situation where c has the responsibility of co-ordinating the activities of each member of the set S. We can assume $c = C(\{c\})$, that is, we assume each member of the organisation co-ordinates his own activities. Clearly if $a = C(\{a, b\})$ and $b = C(\{a, b\})$ then $b = a$. Finally, if $C(\{a, b, c\}) = C(\{C(\{a, b\}), c\})$ we have the associative law, and the relation given by 'co-ordinates' therefore satisfies the axioms of a semilattice (Appendix A). The partial order relation is defined as $a \supseteq b$ if $a = C(\{a, b\})$. If a is superordinate to b then a is responsible for co-ordinating his and b's activities. The co-ordinator of a set of positions corresponds to the least upper bound of the elements corresponding to the set of positions, and the existence of such an element is guaranteed by the structure being a semilattice.

We have then two empirical hypotheses, one which predicts that under certain conditions the organisational structure can be represented by a tree, and one which predicts a semilattice under certain conditions. One difference between the hypotheses stems from the differing superordinate relation for the two hypotheses. Another difference is that in the semilattice, each subset (with at least two elements) has a least common supervisor and the structure ensures control of groups of individuals. As a contrast to this, the tree structure ensures control of individuals.

It is more likely that the prediction of a semilattice will be correct as it is a more general structure. In considering the sociological differences between a semilattice and a tree, it is clear that the co-ordination relation can be qualitatively different in different parts of the structure. Supervisors at level 2 are responsible for individuals in their work unit performing certain tasks. These supervisors are concerned that the work unit produces whatever the company requires. At higher levels, junior and senior management have greater powers of decision and more flexibility in performing their task requirements. Thus some parts of the structure may be a tree (which is still a semilattice) and other parts may have a semilattice (but not a tree) structure. Analysing different substructures with respect to their structural properties will help us to study more closely the reasons for a semilattice structure as opposed to a tree structure.

The distinction between types of structure and the organisational requirements they satisfy should also facilitate study of informal structures in relation to formal structures. Even if hypotheses concerning the formal structure are satisfied, there may be needs that are left unsatisfied which will lead to modifications of the formal structure being made in the informal structure. There is also the possibility that a formal structure does not conform to these hypotheses and modifications in the formal structure lead to the total structure satisfying these hypotheses.

However, the hypothesis of a semilattice structure is a very broad one, and many different structures can satisfy this hypothesis in diverse empirical contexts. One general problem would be to establish conditions for stability of a structure and another would be to study change of organisational structure (both of these within the constraints of a semilattice structure). In terms of the latter, one means of organisational change would be to examine the needs of an organisation at various positions in its structure. For example, if one element c is the least common supervisor of a set of positions S, one manoeuvre to subvert this position would be insert another element between c and all the positions in S. Thus c's control over S is weakened, without having to remove c from the organisation altogether. If two subsets S_1 and S_2, say work units, were in conflict over resources (for example, machine maintenance), one means of controlling this conflict could be to have a specific position c whose responsibility would be to co-ordinate S_1 and S_2. Alternatively S_1 and S_2 could be amalgamated under one least common supervisor.

In order to consider these problems further we need to define a homomorphism. Let $m: S \rightarrow T$ denote a mapping from a semi-lattice S to another semilattice T. The mapping m is said to be order-preserving if $x \subseteq y$ and $m(x) \subseteq m(y)$ (in T) and it is a homomorphism if $m(x \vee y) = m(x) \vee m(y)$ where $x \vee y$ denotes the least upper bound of x and y. If m is a mapping *onto* T then it is called an *epimorphism*, and if it is a 1–1 mapping from S to T it is a *monomorphism*. If both m and m^{-1} exist and are both 1–1 mappings and epimorphisms, then m is an *iso-morphism*. If $S = T$ then m is an *endomorphism*, and finally, if $S = T$ and m is an isomorphism, then it is called an *auto-morphism*.

* A *congruence relation* on a semilattice is an equivalence relation R defined on that semilattice S such that for two elements a and b in the same equivalence class, $a \vee s = b \vee s$ for all $s \in S$. Let S/R denote the set of equivalence (congruence) classes of a congruence relation R defined on a semilattice S. Then we have an epimorphism $\pi: S \rightarrow S/R$ where each element of S is mapped to its congruence class in S/R. It is easily shown that S/R is also a semilattice. Finally an *ideal I* of a semilattice S is a non-empty subset of S with the properties (i) if $a \in I$ and $x \supseteq a$ then $x \in I$, and (ii) if $a \in I$ and $b \in I$ then $a \vee b \in I$.[11]

* Let b be any element of a semilattice S, then $I(b)$ is a *principal ideal* of S where $I(b) = \{x | x \supseteq b\}$. In other words, all the upper bounds of b (together with b) form a principal ideal. We can prove quite straightforwardly that for a finite semilattice every non-empty ideal is a principal ideal, and that for each element of a semilattice there is a corresponding principal ideal. We can prove also that if I is an ideal of a semilattice S, then if we form equivalence classes where a and b belong to the same equivalence class if $a \vee s = b \vee s$ for some $s \in I$, this defines a congruence relation on S (see Appendix A). With these

results we can return to considering the structure of complex organisations as a semilattice.

* The desirability of a semilattice structure (from say the manager's view) stems from the fact that for each subset in the organisation there is a least common superordinate whose role in settling organisational conflict is important. However, organisations are not viewed as one large semilattice of individuals, but rather as a structure made up of groups of positions. The question therefore arises as to whether or not we can provide a rationale for one partition of the organisational structure over some other partition.

* Friedell defines an office-structure as a partition of the elements into offices such that for any two members of the organisation, say a and b, the office of $a \vee b$ is completely determined by the office of a and the office of b. One office, say A, is superordinate to another office B if there is an element $a \in A$ and an element $b \in B$ such that $a \supseteq b$. Every member of a particular office has a superordinate in every superordinate office.

* If we consider an office it is easily shown that it has a unique maximal element, that it is *closed* (if a and $b \in 0$ then $a \vee b \in 0$) and that is convex. (A *convex set* is one where if $a \supseteq c \supseteq b$ and a and b both belong to the set then c does also.) Again it is straightforward to show that a partition of the elements of the semilattice into closed and convex subsets gives a congruence relation where each of these subsets is a congruence class. Thus there is the homomorphism of S onto S/R where R is the congruence relation. It follows from this that the office-structure s also a semilattice.

* Given that the structure of the individuals is a semilattice, an office-structure that is defined in this way is also a semilattice which gives another empirical hypothesis to examine. Clearly a more appropriate approach would be to take the office-structure of an organisation and then examine the individual structure in the light of this. However, there is no reason why the structure of individuals within an office is a semilattice,

whereas in an office-structure constructed in the above fashion, the elements in each office are a semilattice. This too could be an empirical hypothesis with the same arguments applying for each office, as they were applied for the whole structure earlier.

* It is clear also, that given a particular structure of individuals, that in general there can be more than one office structure. In fact, the possible office-structures for a given semilattice of individuals form a lattice. While the hypothesis that the office-structure will be a semilattice is of interest, we may need to establish additional reasons why any one of these structures should be the office-structure. It would be interesting also if there is systematic variation over the size of offices. For example, we might predict that the minimal elements in the office-structure (the work units) are the largest elements, and that further, size of offices varies with the routinisation of the task structure. The maximal element of an office-structure is also of interest as each is an ideal of the original semilattice structure.

There are several lines of enquiry opened by this approach, but it is clear that the initial hypotheses need to be examined before they are extensively built-upon. We need to examine whether organisational strain is caused in formal organisations where the structure is not a semilattice. If it is, then we need to be able to specify which semilattice structure best overcomes this. It is also clear that while sociological reasons can be given for having a semilattice structure in the first place, we do not have such reasons for choosing between semilattice structures. However, this approach is of value for indicating clear structural requirements if certain organisational needs are to be met.

7. Social Status

In most societies, if not all, there exist inequalities between the individuals within them. However, there is a wide dissidence among social theorists as to what is significant about these inequalities. Not only are the problems deemed worthy of study manifold, but the approaches to them are legion. Further, there is an over-abundance of concepts and the same word frequently denotes widely differing concepts. Not surprisingly, there are many theories of stratification. This is not the place to attempt to review the literature (besides, such reviews exist already, for example, Reissman (1967)), but I shall rather focus on particular theoretical problems. Although there are different hierarchical relations present in society their form can be taken to be invariant. This enables us to deal with a wide range of problems within a single formalised perspective.

There is a great deal of debate over what causes the existence of stratification, whether or not it is necessary for society and what its consequences are. In order to tackle any one of these, it appears necessary to presuppose answers to the others. I am concerned here with some of the consequences of stratification and therefore will assume that in a society there are (i) sets of human relations, some of which are hierarchical and some of which are not, (ii) differences with respect to ownership and non-ownership of, or more generally access to, resources and (iii) differences in the ideologies which affect social life. Included among the latter is the range of different perceptions that people can have of the composition of society.[1]

In order to examine how the structure of society enters into the behaviour of individuals through their perception of society, the concept of social consciousness as described by Ossowski is useful. Social consciousness is '. . . an abbreviation to refer to the ideas that characterise certain milieux, for the concepts, images, beliefs and evaluations that are more or less common to people of a certain social environment and which are reinforced in the consciousness of particular individuals by mutual suggestion and by the conviction that they are shared by other people in the same group' (Ossowski, 1963, p. 6). Differing perceptions of the social order by individuals were regarded by Ossowski as important because (i) such perceptions exert an influence on human activity and relations, (ii) we can determine what are regarded by individuals as the important aspects of human relations, (iii) we can achieve insight into a set of human relations through the comparison of differing perceptions of those relations and (iv) they affect social policy and social ideologies.

Another starting point can be made with Weber's concept of status. Status can be defined as the favourable evaluation (or social honour) that a social actor receives from others. Status, therefore, is very much dependent upon the community and is expressed in the judgements of other individuals. The criteria for according status are clearly not unrelated to the varying perceptions of the social order. By starting with a consideration of status, it does not follow that we are necessarily led to the same approach as that of Warner who more or less reduced problems of stratification to issues about status.[2]

Finally, we can also make a start by considering the development of multi-dimensional theories of stratification. It is clear that a variety of characteristics can be used to differentiate individuals. There are, for example, the criteria of age, sex, race and kinship and the criteria of occupation, wealth, income, education or power. Each of these dimensions can be (and has been) used as a major stratification variable. Such usage shares similarities with the way status is conferred, although of course they are not simply reducible to this. Galtung's presentation (particularly Galtung, 1966), of the multi-dimensional approach to stratification is dependent upon the use of mathematics for obtaining measures of the various concepts used in this perspective; for example, status disequilibrium, congruence and criss-cross. His presentation throws up many interesting insights but in common with other discussions (for example Lenski, 1954) it harbours certain fundamental flaws. Some are of a statistical nature (see Blalock, 1967a,b)[3] and some of a conceptual nature (see Doreian and Stockman, 1969). Among the latter is (i) the omission of determining what actually are the rank dimensions operating in a society and (ii) the omission of taking into consideration the manner in which individuals compare their ranks on different dimensions.

A distinction needs to be made between objective social status and subjective social status. 'Subjective' status refers to an individual's belief about his location on particular status dimensions. 'Objective' status refers to where any social scientist would (or could) locate the individual on given criteria.[4] An example of this is the use of a coding scheme for assigning an individual to a social class. The use of such coding schemes often rests upon the assumption that there is consensus over the assignments of status. Frequently this assumption is questionable and it poses severe methodological problems for theorists using the multi-dimensional framework. However, having recognised that stratification is a multi-dimensional phenomenon, it is difficult to justify a research strategy that ignores this. Jackson and Curtis (1968) in their review of part of the stratification literature, suggest that we need precise measures for each independent status component (for stratification research), and (for general sociological research) we need to be able to collapse these into a single theoretically relevant scale. This may well be impossible to achieve, and further, in view of comments in Chapter 3, undesirable. Clearly the selection of a single dimension, say occupation or income, and using it as a single indicator of stratification is inadequate. The discussion of the methodological problems of analysing multi-dimensional phenomena is extraneous to the present discussion, and we turn here to examine particular dimensions which, in the context of stratification, are necessary precursors of such a discussion.

7.1 Assignment of Status[5]

A broad range of cases where status is assigned can be examined within the following framework. Suppose we have a set A of social objects. The elements of this set can be individuals in a natural setting, individuals in an experimental group, social groups like gangs, aggregates like neighbourhoods, social labels like occupation, or even societies. Each of these objects can be described in terms of certain characteristics. In particular, if we have a relevant social variable, the values of that variable can be used to describe the social objects in A. For example, wealth or influence could be used to describe individuals, power to describe gangs, attractiveness to describe neighbourhoods, cleanness to describe occupations and type of political rule to describe societies.

When considering stratification we shall call the variable a stratification characteristic, denote it by C and refer to the values of the variable as states of C. Thus for individuals, we could take C to be income and the states of C as amounts of income. By describing individuals in terms of C we assign each element of A to one of the states of C. Similarly, we could take C to be occupation, and assign elements of A to their corresponding occupational title. It may be possible to define an equivalence relation on the set C, in which case elements of C are grouped together into equivalence classes. In the case of income we could group together values to create income intervals, and in the case of occupations we create occupational groups. We could then define an ordering over the equivalence classes of C. In the case of income, higher incomes are ordered above lower incomes and for occupation we could order the equivalence classes of occupations in terms of, say, importance or even cleanness. In the case of neighbourhoods, we could define C in terms of geographical areas and use the variable attractiveness to order these areas. It is clear that for each of the examples considered so far, the treatment is sufficiently general for it to be applicable. With this said, we shall confine ourselves to the cases of stratification of individuals and of social groups.

In order to continue we shall use the following notation. Let the equivalence relation defined on C be E, and we denote the set of equivalence classes by C/E. The set of equivalence classes is ordered by an asymmetric and transitive order relation P. If P is a complete order, and we shall treat it as such, then for every pair of elements c_1 and c_2 from C exactly one of the following holds c_1Ec_2, c_1Pc_2, c_2Pc_1.

The description of elements in A by elements in C can be represented by a mapping from A to C; $c: A \rightarrow C$, and we have also the mapping $\pi: C \rightarrow C/E$ where π maps each element to its equivalence class. Clearly πc (c followed by π) is a mapping from A to C/E, $\pi c: A \rightarrow C/E$ and denotes the assignment of status to each element of A. We are assuming also that C/E contains at least two elements. If it did not, then the whole of C would be an equivalence class. This would amount to C not differentiating between individuals, and not being a status characteristic.[6]

The ordering that has been defined on C/E can arise in any number of ways. If A is a set of respondents in a survey, then this order could be one used by a sociologist studying the population from which the sample was drawn. If A was a set of neighbourhoods, the ordering of geographical areas could be that constructed by a couple looking for a house. (In this case, we could take A to be a set of houses and C the neighbourhoods surrounding the houses.) Finally if A is a set of individuals then each member of A can create their own ordering of C, which can then be used by the individual to describe all the individuals in A.

Recalling that status is based on the evaluation of others, we shall now restrict our attention to the case where A is a set of individuals, C is a status dimension and both the equivalence relation E and the order relation P are defined by the individuals of A. Now the order relation P can be taken as a preference order in which case the elements of C/E are indifference classes (that is, there is no preference between elements of the same class) and C/E is completely ordered. In this case, we can also represent the elements of C/E on an ordinal scale. We then can map C/E into the set of real numbers R, where the ordering of R is the only significant feature of R. (It may sometimes be the case that the elements of C/E form an algebra, for example, a semilattice for status in an organisation, in which case we would map C/E into an appropriate algebra.) In general, we shall map into R (using whatever properties of R that are appropriate) and we use r to denote the 1–1 mapping $r: C/E \rightarrow R$. Then $r\pi c$ is a mapping, $r\pi c: A \rightarrow R$. We denote this by s, and with Fararo, term it a status chain, $s = A \overset{c}{\rightarrow} C \overset{\pi}{\rightarrow} C/E \overset{r}{\rightarrow} R$.

Suppose that we have two status chains s_1 and s_2 where $s_1: A \rightarrow E_1$ and $s_2: A \rightarrow E_2$, where R_1 and R_2 denote algebras. If there is a homomorphic mapping $m: R_1 \rightarrow R_2$ such that $ms_1 = s_2$, then the two chains are homomorphic. If, furthermore, m is an isomorphism then the two chains are isomorphic. Suppose, for example, R_1 is an ordinal scale of numbers and m is an order-preserving mapping from R_1 to R_2, then the two chains are isomorphic as the relevant scale properties are preserved. If R_1 is an interval scale and m a linear transformation of that scale that maps R_1 to R_2, then the two status chains are isomorphic. (In the latter case, if m was not linear the two status chains would not be isomorphic).

The discussion so far has made no allowance for the individuals of A having differing status mappings and assigning status differently to each other. Let a denote any element of A, then for every $a \in A$ we can have $c_a: A \rightarrow C$ and $\pi_a: C \rightarrow C/E_a$. We are assuming that for each status characteristic C, everybody recognises the same states of C, but we are not assuming that they all create the same equivalence classes.[7] In the case of income, some people might recognise many income groups while others might only use gross income categories. Moreover, there may be differences as to which categories exist and how they are defined. This is what Ossowski noted to be of great importance; individuals having different perceptions of the stratification of a group of actors A. We have in this case a set of status chains $\{s_a\}$ where each status chain is that defined by an individual $a \in A$. By formalising the study of status in this fashion places us in a position to examine and compare different assignments of status (status chains).

If the individuals of A all agree on the characterisation of A in terms of C, that is, if $c_a = c_b$ for any $a, b \in A$, then the set of status chains are cognitively uniform and we refer to this as a case of cognitive uniformity. If they all agree on how the status of C are evaluated ($\pi_a = \pi_b$ for any $a, b \in A$), then the set of status chains are evaluatively uniform and we call this a case of evaluative uniformity. Simultaneous cognitive and evaluative uniformity is referred to simply as uniformity. If $c_a = c_b$ and $\pi_a = \pi_b$ for all $a, b \in A$, it is clear that $\pi_a c_a = \pi_b c_b$, but while these are sufficient conditions for the status mappings to be the same, they are not necessary conditions for this. It is possible to have different c_a's and different π_a's and still have equivalent status assignments.[8]

For example, suppose C is the variable income and the states of are $\{C_1, C_2, \ldots C_a\}$ where (in pounds sterling say) $C_1 =$ over 4,000, $C_2 = 3{,}000{-}3{,}999$, $C_3 = 2{,}500{-}2{,}999$, $C_4 = 2{,}000{-}2{,}499$, $C_5 = 1{,}700{-}1{,}999$, $C_6 = 1{,}400{-}1{,}699$, $C_7 = 1{,}000{-}1{,}399$, $C_8 = 700{-}999$ and $C_9 =$ under 700. Now suppose we have three individuals a, b and d whose respective incomes are (in pounds) 3,500, 1,800 and 900. Now if they each know each other's incomes, then each individual will map a to C_2, b to C_5 and d to C_8. In this case, $c_a(a) = c_b(a) = c_d(a)$ and similarly for b and d. Suppose however they are required to simply determine incomes as high, medium and low, and that according to a, High = 3,000 and over, Medium 1,700–2,999 and Low is under 1,700. We denote these by H_a, M_a and L_a respectively. Similarly, we may have $H_b = 2{,}500$ and over, $M_b = 1{,}400{-}2{,}499$ and

L_b = under 1,400; and H_d = 2,000 and over, M_d = 1,000–1,999 and L_d = under 1,000. It is clear that a, b and d have created different equivalence classes. However $\pi_a c_a(a)$ = 'High' as does $\pi_b c_b(a)$ and $\pi_d c_d(a)$. Similarly b and d are mapped to Medium and Low respectively. Suppose now that a, b and d estimate the incomes of each other. In this case it is possible, perhaps likely, that they will differ in their estimates of each other's income. For the individual we have labelled a, $c_a(a)$ can be C_1, C_2 or C_3 without changing the final categorisation. For b, $c_b(a)$ can be any of C_1 to C_4 and for d, $c_d(a)$ can be any of C_1 to C_5 without changing the placing of a in the final coding scheme. Finally we could drop the assumption of C being a characteristic with the same states, and still have the mapping from A to C/I_a the same for each individual although clearly there are differing mappings used to give the final product of mappings. In these cases the end result is the same; there is consensus over the final states, although there are differing paths to this consensus.

It is clear from the examples of the preceding paragraph that there is some latitude in specifying the component mappings (within the restriction that the outcome of the mappings is the same). More formally this can be stated (Fararo, 1968, p. 183) that if a set of status chains for a given A and a given C, are evaluatively uniform, and if for each pair of status chains s_a and s_b the characterisations c_a and c_b differ only within E-equivalent states, the status chains are all isomorphic.[9]

In the multi-dimensional theories of stratification, a crucial assumption is that status dimensions are compared. In the experimental work discussed by Berger et al. (1966) high status on one dimension tended to carry over onto other dimensions. It is clear that we need a way of discussing the comparison of status dimensions. Suppose then we have two status chains, corresponding to two status dimensions and defined by one individual of A.[10] (See Figure 7.1. The letter subscripts are dropped, but this is not to assume uniformity.)

Suppose we attempt to map C_1/E_1 to C_2/E_2. We can always do this, but we are only interested in particular mappings. The individual whose status chains are shown in Figure 7.1 may attempt to compare the two dimensions in terms of their consistency. In other words, for each element of C_1/E_1, there is

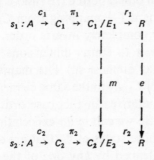

Figure 7.1

one element (or possibly more) that is consistent with this in C_2/E_2. If education and income are the two status characteristics then for each level of education there may be an appropriate income group. All other pairs of elements, one taken from C_1/E_1 and one from C_2/E_2, are inconsistent in the sense of the

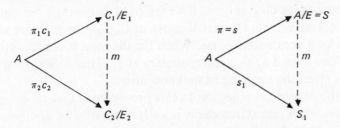

Figure 7.2 Computative status chain diagrams

rank theorists. Such mappings, m, represent beliefs about the relation between status dimensions. The rationale for this procedure is perhaps clearer if one dimension concerns performance of particular tasks and we are attempting to choose appropriate levels in terms of individuals' experience or training as the other status dimension.

Consider the diagrams of Figure 7.2 where 7.2(a) represents the case we are talking about. Now if the mapping $\pi_1 c_1: A \to C_2/E_2$ is such that for every element $a \in A$, $m\pi_1 c(a) = \pi_2 c_2(a)$ the diagram is a *commutative diagram* and the two chains are consistent with each other, both C_1/E_1 and C_2/E_2 are completely ordered, and if m is a 1–1 mapping from C_1/E_1 to C_2/E_2 that preserves order, or completely inverts order. (The latter is not different with respect to status dimensions as we can always re-order a particular dimension.) The mapping m might map different elements of C_1/E_1 to the same element in C_2/E_2 making the diagram commutative. In this case order is not fully preserved. In every case we call m an expectation, as it associates with states of C_1 those states of C_2 that are expected to be consistent with it, as defined by any one of the individuals of A.

Now it does not follow that for every situation like that of Figure 7.2(a) (where m is the expectation mapping) that the diagram is commutative. If we regard one status dimension as a model of the other, we could try and determine the states of the second dimension simply from those of the first dimension and m, without any reference to $\pi_2 c_2$. If we successfully do this, it is clear that the diagram (like that of Figure 7.2(a)) will be a commutative diagram, and if we fail (that is, the expected states do not agree with the actual states of C_2/E_2), the diagram will not be a commutative one. When the diagram is commutative we can regard s_1 as a *representation* of s_2. That is, knowing s_1 and given the mapping m we know also s_2.

The immediate objection to this procedure is that we do not know when one status chain is a representative of another. It is all right to talk of commutative diagrams, but there is no guarantee that an individual will perceive or regard dimensions in this way. In general we know s_1 and s_2. The empirical question is whether or not an m exists, which changes the problem we are discussing. We know that E is an equivalence relation defined on the set C which partitions C. Indirectly this also partitions A. Every element of A that is mapped to any element contained in a particular equivalence class of C/E will belong in the same equivalence class in the induced partition of A. This set of equivalence classes we denote by A/E. Now in Figure 7.2(b) we have represented mappings from A to a status characteristic S and from A to A/E. (If we were to use C and C/E the following argument would still hold, but it would involve discussing the status chains of two individuals. We go on to do this, but we are still concerned with two status mappings of a single individual.) We can specify conditions under which the required m exists.

* Let A and B be sets, $C(A)$ the set of equivalence relations definable on A and $M(A, B)$ the set of mappings from A to B. We have the following results:[11]

1. If $p \in M(A)$ then $p^{-1}p \in C(A)$. In other words, $p^{-1}p$ is an equivalence relation on A.

2. Let $E \in C(A)$ and $p \in M(A, B)$ such that $p^{-1}p \subseteq E$ then there exists a unique mapping $q: A/E \to B$ such that $q\pi = p$ (where $\pi: A \to A/E$ is the epimorphism mapping each a to its equivalence class).

3. If p is a mapping from A onto B such that $p^{-1}p = E$ then p induces an isomorphism $q: A/E \to B$.

These results, if instead of B we use S_1, and if instead of p and q we use s_1 and m respectively, apply directly to Figure 7.2(b).

Now there are many status dimensions which could be used to differentiate people belonging to a given society. It is clear from the previous discussion that we are interested in selecting particular dimensions that play a special role among the many possible dimensions. The significance of these status dimensions is that they can be used as models of other status dimensions. We will be looking at two kinds of dimension, *diffuse* dimensions and *status symbols* (Fararo, 1969). It will become clear that they can each be represented abstractly in diagrams like figure 7.2(b), although they have differences in terms of processes of stratification.

If we now ask what a status symbol is (again in the mind of one individual) it is a visible means by which he can infer ranks on other status dimensions, given that he observes a particular level of a status symbol. For example, ownership of a large house, an expensive car or a boat can be taken as indicators of high wealth, a high income and a certain style of life. The idea of conspicuous consumption is clearly related and this too could be taken (during one period of time at least) as a status symbol. We can define a status symbol by recapitulation of the above argument and the theorem given, by saying that the pair (S, s) form a status symbol of S_1 for an actor of A if and only if there is a mapping m from S to S_1 such that $ms = s_1$. The subscripts have been omitted thus far as we were dealing with a particular individual of A. By re-introducing subscripts we could discuss status symbols according to how individuals see and use them. If we assume cognitive and evaluative uniformity, then the definition of a status symbol applies for all the members of A. On the other hand, if we cannot make this assumption, there arises the possibility of different subgroups having different status symbols or a case where there is a common status symbol representing different dimensions according to who is using the status symbol.

It is clear that the structure of the diagrams for the expectation mapping is exactly that of the diagrams for status symbols. The idea of a diffuse status is based on expectations. A diffuse dimension is one that 'spills over' on to other dimensions. Rather than spell out in detail how a status dimension operates as a diffuse dimension, it is sufficient to say that a diffuse dimension symbolises many dimensions. A status dimension C is a diffuse status dimension over A (assuming uniformity) if there are many status dimensions C_i existing with the required expectation maps $m_i: S \to C_i/E_i$. The context in which this notion has been developed is one of experiments concerning status in a small group. As it has been presented here, it would apply either to small groups or to large communities. Sometimes the distinction is not important, but for many problems the distinction must be maintained.

If we consider the various dimensions of a potential multi-dimensional model (that is, a finite set of socially relevant dimensions),[12] rather than pick out the diffuse statuses, we could possibly order the dimensions with respect to their diffuseness. Thus in Figure 7.3 the dimensions C_1 to C_k are ordered according to their diffuseness which is only one possibility out of many.

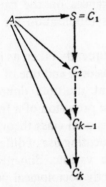

Figure 7.3

Another would be that the dimensions cluster into distinct subsets of dimensions, with each ordered according to the diffuseness of their status dimensions. In general, such tidy orderings may be impossible to achieve and we are left with the full multi-dimensional problem: attempting to map $C_1 \times C_2 \times \cdots \times C_k$ into the real numbers or other measurement systems. Fararo's suggestion of obtaining a lexicographic ordering and Galtung's (1964) suggestion that the dimensions might form a Guttman scale (see Guttman, 1949 or Torgerson, 1958) are both attempts to obtain an easy way out of this dilemma by ordering the dimensions.

Even if this ordering is not obtainable, it may be possible to pull out key dimensions in the sense that they are diffuse. In this case it is necessary to exercise care as to how the diffuse dimension is being used. In the case of a small group (experimental or otherwise) it is probably quite legitimate simply to focus on status. In the case of much larger aggregates to focus on a status symbol is again legitimate. However, there may be dimensions that are causally prior to others, and it would be misleading to describe them as simply symbolising these other dimensions. If it was possible to have a single dimension, denoting class in say the Marxist sense, that is causally prior to other dimensions, differences on these other dimensions are dependent upon differences on the causally prior dimension which is not a mere symbolisation for the dependent dimensions.

However, class is frequently taken as a heterogeneous collection of confused dimensions, and one of the theoretically useful reasons for looking at multiple dimensions, as Landecker (1960) points out, is the provision of a framework within which the merits of unidimensional class theories could be compared with those theories advocating use of different status dimensions. By analysing how the various dimensions enter into social consciousness, the strictly sociological perspective provided by the set theoretical analysis of Fararo is, potentially at least, fruitful.

7.2 Stratification Systems

The conceptualisation outlined in the previous section can be used in different ways. Fararo (1969) considers the action within a small experimental group as it attempts to perform certain tasks. The individuals making up this group may be ranked on a status dimension that is directly relevant to the performance of the task. If their rankings on this dimension were known to the group, they would know which individual had the required expertise and take up his suggestions. If on the other hand they did not have this knowledge, or no such dimension existed, the group would have to activate other status dimensions. Those dimensions which order the individuals would be of interest, but not in a fashion that was directly relevant to the task at hand. These dimensions would be called diffuse status dimensions if the rankings on them were used to evaluate the utility of suggestions for performing the task according to who makes these suggestions. The diffuse dimensions and the experimental work which prompted the analysis of such dimensions are discussed in Berger et al. (1966). If, however, status dimensions were related to each other according to balance theory, Fararo's treatment of these dimensions is a generalisation to the case of more than two 'ranks' on the dimension.

An alternative way in which this outline can be used is to consider stratification systems (Fararo, 1970). Here certain features, among them the finiteness of A and the existence of status characteristics together with corresponding status chains, can be stated as axioms and the properties of the stratification system deduced. By different sets of properties different stratification systems can be constructed and then compared. The importance of this is two-fold. On the one hand we can consider particular stratificational systems that we can observe and compare their properties. On the other hand, we can construct hypothetical systems (or rather, other possible systems) and study their properties. The analysis of status as initiated by Fararo, and outlined briefly in this chapter, facilitates the study of a wide range of topics in stratification. Moreover, this is done within a single framework and as such provides a promising basis for a mathematical analysis of stratification.

8. Social Mobility

Galtung in his introductory work on theory and methods in social research (Galtung, 1967) describes social behaviour as behaviour in space and time. However, the majority of sociological studies tend to ignore time and tend to study cross-sections in time. Frequently the cost of research imposes this limitation, but such studies have to be predicated on the assumption that conditions of equilibrium prevail. Studies of processes through time are not so frequent and often we lack the terminology to describe these processes of social change. There are mathematical areas that are ideally suited to describing change: differential equations and difference equations. Both explicitly include time, but they are, however, beyond the scope of this book,[1] although their use has been suggested for sociological analysis (Coleman, 1964,[2] 1968 and Goldberg, 1957).

8.1 Mobility and Stratification

Social mobility is by definition change over time, and the study of social mobility is one attempt to analyse social processes. In many respects however, the conventional framework of the social mobility table represents a compromise between the many demands of analysis through time and the limitations imposed by cross-sectional methods of data collection (and concepts similarly restricted). However, a start can be made in dealing with the conceptual problems of social change. Changes over time are studied by comparing 'spatial distributions' at different points in time. Social mobility is a social process whereby individuals may move through a social structure, and where the structure can also be transformed. Suppose the population of a society can be partitioned into mutually exclusive and exhaustive categories. In conventional analyses of social mobility these categories are taken to be occupational categories, and for migration the categories are geographical regions. The categories need to be relevant to the way a society operates, and the hierarchical relations imposed by the means of production are central: stratification, social mobility and social structure are closely connected. In this context we can talk of social structure as the distribution of individuals, and groups of individuals, into a hierarchy of positions created by stratification. Relations like control over, superiority to, and manipulation of, are defined on the set of positions. Another qualitatively different relation can be defined on the categories, namely, movement between categories. This movement is defined (for stratificational categories) as social mobility, and among the factors affecting social mobility are the social relations defined on the hierarchy of positions.

Subsequently the (so-called) basic model is described in abstract terms. As such, it is applicable to many different types of movement. First we consider some of the theoretical problems that can be studied under the rubric of social mobility. These can be construed as making up three broad classes of problems: (i) What is social mobility and how can we characterise it? (ii) What are the causes of social mobility? (iii) What are the consequences of social mobility? The first of these three is basically methodological and is of fundamental importance. If we have widely differing ideas as to what social mobility is then we are talking about different concepts. If social mobility is regarded as movement between categories, then by differing choices of categories and different definitions of movement, completely different mobility processes can be described.[3]

For an individual, mobility is movement between categories and immobility is remaining in the same category. There are many questions we can ask: What motivated the individual to be mobile? What was the consequence of his mobility in terms of,

E

say, his attitudes? What was the effect of mobility on the hierarchical relations? Is there a disruption of these and other social relations or does the mobile individual fit smoothly into a new pattern of such relations? If we consider the structure of categories, does the cumulative effect of mobility of many individuals change this structure? Alternatively, we can ask whether the structure precludes social mobility and maintains dominance relations.

In order to pose these questions and begin to answer them we need (minimally) to be able to say whether mobility exists or whether it does not. At first sight it might appear that this is all we need and that, methodologically, this is sufficient to examine hypotheses like 'social mobility causes . . .' or '. . . causes social mobility.' However, in a hierarchy of positions, direction of mobility has to be considered. If we can talk of experiencing limited or great social mobility, then we need to be able to discriminate between amounts of social mobility. We need also to be able to talk of the rapidity of social movement. Upward mobility achieved slowly over considerable time may affect an individual differently from rapid social mobility. Large amounts of social mobility may have different effects than small amounts. Upward mobility may differ in its effects from downward mobility. While a description of mobility is certainly not the end product of research into mobility, little can be said without it.

Instead of focusing attention upon individuals, we can also consider the whole social structure. We need to obtain measures of mobility for this also. If the social structure itself is changing there is a minimal amount of social mobility that must occur. What can we say if more than this minimum amount of mobility occurs? If one social structure is radically transformed while another remains unchanged, but the amount of individual mobility in each structure is the same, are there differences between the structures in terms of the social mobility within each? But first we need to clear the ground in order to be able to make such comparisons.

8.2 The Basic Model

Suppose in a given society we have k categories into which a population can be placed. Let the size of the population be N and let the number of people in the ith category be n_i. The distribution of individuals into the categories can be written as a vector $(n_1, n_2 \cdots, n_k)$ where $\sum_{i=1}^{k} n_i = N$. Clearly the proportion in the ith category will be $a_i = n_i/N$ and these proportions can also be written as a vector $a = (a_1, a_2 \cdots, a_k)$ where $\sum_{i=1}^{k} a_i = 1$. Suppose further that this is the distribution at time t_0, and that at some subsequent time t_1 the respective distributions are $(m_1, m_2 \cdots, m_k)$ and $\beta = (b_1, b_2 \cdots, b_k)$ where $\sum_{i=1}^{k} m_i = M = N$, and $b_i = m_i/M$. Social mobility is studied by considering how the distribution a is transformed to the distribution β (which is not necessarily different from a).

Having stated the problem in these precise terms, implicit assumptions can be made readily clear. The first of these is that the population might be closed.[4] Clearly $M = N$ is not incompatible with some individuals leaving the structure and others entering it, but in most analyses of mobility, the assumption of a closed population is made. It can, however, be dispensed with (see below). Another assumption is that there is the same number of categories at t_1 as there are at t_0. Normally a further assumption that the categories at t_1 and at t_0 are the same is made. This clearly is an empirical problem, and the assumption can be dropped although to do this will preclude use of certain techniques.[5] One less stringent assumption would be that the two distributions are comparable in so far as one could be obtained from the other by collapsing categories. Another assumption that is usually made, although not apparent thus far, is that the ordering of the categories remains unchanged in the interval $(t_1 - t_0)$.

Let n_{ij} denote the number of individuals in the ith category at time t_0 who are in the jth category at time t_1. Consider now the individuals in the ith category at t_0. Denote the number[6] of them by n_i· and denote by n_{ij} the number of these that end up in the jth category at t_1. Clearly this can be done for each of the categories and we have k^2 numbers like n_{ij}. Similarly for $p_{ij} = n_{ij}/N$, where p_{ij} denotes the proportion of individuals (in N) who were in the ith category at t_0 and the jth category at t_1. Consider now the matrix $P = [p_{ij}]$ and the post-multiplication of α by P, which gives another vector (see Appendix C). Consider now the first element of this vector, $a_1p_{11} + a_2p_{21} + \cdots + a_kp_{k1}$. This clearly is the proportion of individuals who end up in the first category at time t_1, and similarly for each other category. In other words, we have the matrix equation:

$$\beta = \alpha P.$$

This is the fundamental matrix equation for mobility analysis (Matras, 1967) which expresses the transformation of α into β by a process represented by P. This matrix equation represents a set of k equations:[7]

$$b_i = a_1p_{1i} + a_2p_{2i} + \cdots + a_kp_{ki}, \quad 1 \leqslant i \leqslant k$$

These equations can be used to write out the so-called mobility table. Three versions are presented in Table 8.1, one for the actual numbers (n_{ij}), one for proportions (p_{ij}) and one for conditional proportions ($p_{ij}' = p_{ij}/p_i. = n_{ij}/n_i.$).

TABLE 8.1 Equivalent forms of the social mobility table

Distribution at t_1

n_{11}	n_{12}	.	.	n_{1k}	$n_1.$
n_{21}	n_{22}	.	. .	n_{2k}	$n_2.$
.	.			.	.
.	.			.	.
n_{k1}	n_{k2}	.	. .	n_{kk}	$n_k.$
$n._1$	$n._2$	.	. .	$n._k$	N

Distribution at t_0

$$\sum_{=1}^{k} n_{ij} = n_i \quad \sum_{i=1}^{k} n_{ij} = n_{\cdot j} \text{ and } \sum_{i=1}^{k} n_{i\cdot} = \sum_{=1}^{k} n_{\cdot j} = N$$

(a) Matrix $N = [\ n_{ij}\ ]$

Distribution at t_1

	p_{11}	p_{12}	.	.	.	p_{1k}	$p_{1\cdot}$
	p_{21}	p_{22}	.	.	.	p_{2k}	$p_{2\cdot}$
Distribution at t_0	.	.				.	.
	.	.				.	.
	p_{k1}	p_{k2}	.	.	.	p_{kk}	$p_{k\cdot}$
	$p_{\cdot 1}$	$p_{\cdot 2}$	.	.	.	$p_{\cdot k}$	1

$$\sum_{i}^{k} p_{ij} = p_{i\cdot}, \ \sum_{i}^{k} p_{ij} = p_{\cdot j} \text{ and } \sum_{j}^{k} p_{i\cdot} = \sum^{k} p_{\cdot j} = 1$$

(b) Matrix $P = [\ p_{ij}\ ]$

Distribution at t_1

	p'_{11}	p'_{12}	.	.	.	p'_{1k}	1
	p'_{21}	p'_{22}	.	.	.	p'_{2k}	1
Distribution at $t/$	.	.				.	.
	.	.				.	.
	p'_{k1}	p'_{k2}	.	.	.	p'_{kk}	1
							k

$$\sum_{=1}^{k} p'_{ij} = 1$$

(c) †Matrix of p'_{ij}

† Note that there is no marginal distributions for column sums of the p'_{ij}. We could construct this matrix so that $p'_{ij} = p_{ij}/p_{\cdot j}$ and $\sum p'_{ij} = 1$. In this case, there would be no a priori marginal distribution for row sums.

8.3 Gross Mobility, Net Mobility and Exchange Mobility

It is clear that given α and given β, the matrix P is not unique. In other words, more than one process could transform the structure of α to that of β. We need to know the properties of α, β and P in order to obtain parameters that characterise the mobility process. Some of these parameters are:

(i) proportion of the ith category mobile,

$$P_{Mi} = \sum_{j \neq i} p'_{ij} = 1 - p'_{ii}$$

(this makes no reference to any ordering of the categories, and applies whether or not such an ordering exists),

(ii) proportion of the ith category upwardly mobile,[8]

$$P_{Ui} = \sum_j p'_{ij} \quad \text{for} \quad i < j$$

(iii) proportion of the ith category downwardly mobile,

$$P_{Di} = \sum_j p'_{ij} \quad \text{for} \quad i > j$$

(iv) proportion of the ith category immobile, $P_{Ii} = p'_{ii}$

Clearly   (a) $P_{Mi} = P_{Ui} + P_{Di}$

and   (b) $P_{Mi} + P_{Ii} = 1$

(v) Total proportion of the population mobile,

$$P_M = 1 - \sum p_i p'_{ii}$$

Equivalently $P_M = \sum p_{ij}, i \neq j, P_M = 1 - \sum_i p_{ii}$

(vi) Total proportion of the population immobile $P_I = 1 - P_M$.

We can obtain similar proportions of the total population that is upwardly or downwardly mobile. The proportion P_M represents the gross mobility. In terms of Table 8.1(a), the total number of individuals mobile is $N - \sum_i n_{ii} = \sum_{\substack{i,i \\ i \neq j}} n_{ij}$ and as a proportion of N this is $1 - \sum_i p_{ii}$. Gross mobility, together with net and exchange mobility and the relation between all three is made clear if we consider particular mobility tables.

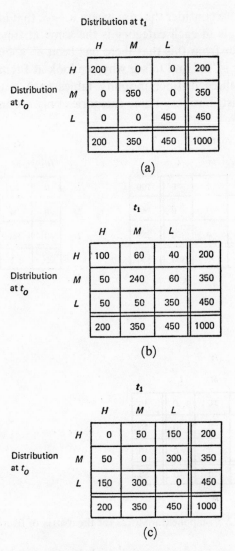

Figure 8.1 Mobility tables with identical marginal distributions (a) No mobility at all (b) Partial exchange mobility (c) Exchange mobility only

Suppose we consider the case where $\alpha = \beta$, that is the number of individuals in each category is the same at time t_1 as at t_0. Can we infer from this that there has been no social mobility? The answer is 'no' and to see why, we look at Figure 8.1 which represents three distinct mobility tables each with the same marginal distributions. Three categories only are used and, for

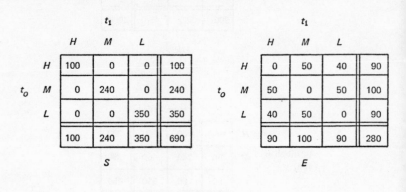

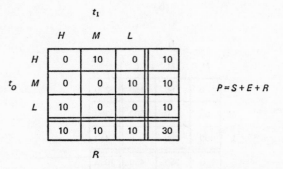

Figure 8.2 Component matrices for the matrix of figure 8.1 (b)

convenience only, they are labelled H, M, L (high, medium, low). In Figure 8.1(a) there is no mobility of any kind. In Figure 8.1(c) there is no immobility, but all the mobility is such that for each pair of categories the flow in one direction is the same as the flow in the other direction; there is only exchange mobility. Figure 8.1(b) shows that some individuals are immobile and given this together with the marginal distributions means that mobility must take place. Exchange mobility can

t_1

		H	M	L	
	H	110	70	20	200
t_0	M	30	310	60	400
	L	10	220	170	400
		150	600	250	1000

(a)

t_1

		H	M	L	
	H	110	0	0	110
t_0	M	0	310	0	310
	L	0	0	170	170
		110	310	170	590

S

t_1

		H	M	L	
	H	0	30	10	40
t_0	M	30	0	60	90
	L	10	60	0	70
		40	90	70	200

E

0	40	10	50
0	0	0	0
0	160	0	160
0	200	10	210

R

Figure 8.3 (a) Mobility matrix P with distinct marginal distribution
(b) Component matrices of P

E*

account for some of this mobility and the remainder is called residual mobility.

The net mobility is defined solely in terms of the marginal distributions. For each category i, the minimum mobility required to change n_i to m_i is $\frac{1}{2}|n_i - m_i|$ and for the whole table the net mobility is $\Sigma \frac{1}{2}|n_i - m_i|$. Let P denote the mobility matrix and S, E and R denote the immobility matrix, the exchange mobility matrix and the residual matrix respectively. It is clear that $P = S + E + R$. Figure 8.2 shows these component matrices for the mobility matrix of Figure 8.1(b).

Any mobility matrix can be broken down into these component matrices. Figure 8.3(b) shows the breakdown for the matrix of Figure 8.3(a) whose marginal distributions are not equal. Both of the matrices S and E are necessarily symmetric matrices. There are k entries in the matrix R, but these are not confined to a single entry in each row and column. The gross mobility matrix is given by $G = (E + R)$, and the basic equation can be expressed in terms of the component matrices;[9] $\alpha P = \alpha(S + G) = \alpha(S + E + R) = \beta$. There is no matrix corresponding to the net mobility as it is constructed from the marginal distributions only. Whenever there is no gross mobility there is no net mobility (see Figure 8.1(a)), but zero net mobility does not necessarily entail zero gross mobility (see Figure 8.1(c)).

The indices described at the beginning of the chapter can be refined slightly by considering the component matrices. Frequently however, distinctions are not made between the various 'types' of mobility. (This is particularly so with the indices considered in the following section.) It is not hard to imagine that matrices P having widely differing component matrices are representing qualitatively different mobility processes. This is true also of the distinction between gross and net mobility, which can be seen to hinge on the notion of exchange mobility (see below). Ramsøy (1966) considered a mobility matrix for Norwegian data, when broken down into mobility matrices for particular areas. These areas ranged from the capital Oslo, to remote fishing villages.[10] She found differing mobility patterns in the different areas. The industrial area was characterised by a high gross mobility but with very little net mobility, whereas for the fishing villages, the gross mobility was made up mainly by high net mobility. The latter structure was changing (with little exchange mobility) whereas the former structure was not changing (but there was considerable exchange mobility). The single (collapsed) national mobility table was hiding significant variation in regional mobility patterns. Such differences need to be checked before attempting to analyse a single national mobility table. If considerable regional variation is shown to exist the national table becomes a near meaningless construct.

8.4 Indices of Mobility

We have already considered some of the more frequently used indices in the previous section, namely the index of net mobility and the proportions of the population that are mobile in a particular way. These measures are obtained from the size of the structural categories or from individual cells. An alternative procedure is to construct a base line and measure mobility in terms of departure from this base line. Two obvious base lines would be those for a completely immobile society or a completely mobile society. Suppose we consider the latter. How would a completely mobile society be defined?

Conventionally this is taken to be a society where everybody has the same chance of reaching a particular category.[11] In other words, the category that an individual belongs to at time t_1 is independent of the category he belonged to at time t_0. Broadly speaking this means social origins have no effect on social mobility. Thus far the discussion has been couched in terms of a given population and its mobility through time. This corresponds to intra-generational mobility where the two marginal distributions in a mobility table are distributions of a given set of individuals. We can also consider the inter-generational mobility table, where the distribution at t_0 is a distribution of fathers, and the distribution at t_1 is the distribution of their sons. In this sense, the population is made up of family lines instead of individuals. We shall see that study of the latter is beset by crucial methodological difficulties. We can continue our discussion with either type of mobility in mind. Social origins can refer to father's position for inter-generational mobility, and to an individual's position at an earlier time in the case of intra-generational mobility.

The idea that an individual's current position is independent of his own (or his father's) previous position is called the perfect mobility hypothesis. Mathematically this is the same as if the mobility table were an ordinary contingency table and conditions of statistical independence prevailed. Suppose we know the two marginal distributions $(n_1., n_2., \ldots n_k.)$ and $(n._1, n._2, \ldots n._k)$. Then under conditions of perfect mobility the expected value of the (i, j) cell would be $\dfrac{n_i. n._j}{N}$. Figure 8.4 shows the mobility table P (of Figure 8.3) together with the corresponding perfect mobility table.

Distribution at t_1

	H	M	L	
H	110	70	20	200
M	30	310	60	400
L	10	220	170	400
	150	600	250	1000

(a)

	H	M	L	
H	30	120	50	200
M	60	240	100	400
L	60	240	100	400
	150	600	250	1000

(b)

	H	M	L
H	3.7	0.6	0.4
M	0.5	1.6	0.6
L	0.2	0.9	1.7

(c)

Figure 8.4 Perfect mobility (a) Mobility table P (b) Perfect mobility table (c) Matrix of mobility ratios

In conventional analyses, the mobility table is compared cell by cell with the values obtained using the perfect mobility hypothesis. For each all the ratio

$$R_{ij} = \frac{\text{observed value}}{\text{expected value}} = \frac{n_{ij}N}{n_i.n.}$$

is calculated and these are called mobility ratios. Even though the use of mobility ratios has been widespread there has been considerable debate about their utility. Billewicz (1955) criticised these measures while Scott (1955) defended them and Durbin (1955) constructed an alternative measure. This debate was repeated nearly a decade later when Yasuda (1964) provided criticism of the mobility ratios, and presented an alternative measure, and Gross (1964) defended them.

The basic limitation of the R_{ij} is that they are not independent of the marginal distributions and consequently do not have a fixed range. In the case of perfect mobility R_{ij} has the value 1. However, if $n_i. > n._j$ then $\max(R_{ij}) = N/n._j$ and if $n._i > n_j.$ then $\max(R_{ji}) = N/n_j.$. A further criticism is made by Blau and Duncan (1967). They prove the elementary but important result that a matrix of mobility ratios imply unique marginal distributions for the corresponding mobility table.

The usual pattern of mobility ratios is that they have values greater than 1 on the main diagonal and values smaller than 1 elsewhere in the table. Thus the perfect mobility hypothesis under-predicts the number of cases remaining in the same category. However, Goodman (1969b) demonstrates that this cannot be readily interpreted. He suggests alternative procedures based upon his 'quasi-perfect' mobility hypothesis (Goodman, 1965, 1969b). If certain cells are blanked out then the remainder of the table will conform to perfect mobility. Initially Goodman considers the diagonal cells as being blanked out. Thus the quasi-perfect mobility hypothesis would, in this case, predict that once individuals move from their initial categories the movement conforms to perfect mobility. His procedure can be generalised to blank out any cells in a table. In this manner the quasi-perfect mobility hypothesis provides a more useful baseline for the construction of indices to measure features of mobility and immobility.[12]

*8.5 Stochastic Models of Mobility

A stochastic process is intuitively a time-dependent probability process. These can be classified into four classes given by discrete or continuous time and discrete or continuous state space. We will consider here only those with discrete time and discrete state space.[13] A Markov process is a stochastic process characterised by a set of k states $S = \{S_i\}$, a probability distribution $\{B(t)\}$ over the states at each time, where $B(t) = [b_i(t)]$ and a square matrix $P(t) = [p_{ij}(t)]$. The element $b_i(t)$ is the probability that at a time t an element is in the ith category S_i, $1 \leqslant i \leqslant k$. Each $b_i(t)$ is a real, non-negative number and is restricted to the range $0 \leqslant b_i(t) = 1$ (for each i) and $\Sigma_i \, b_i(t) = 1$. The matrix entry $p_{ij}(t)$ is the probability that an element in state S_i at time $t - 1$ will be in state S_j at time t. In other words, each $p_{ij}(t)$ is a conditional probability. In a Markov process the outcome at time t is dependent only upon the outcome at time $t - 1$, and on no previous outcome.

Suppose now that our k categories correspond to the set of states. At a given time t, $B(t)$ is a probability distribution giving the probability that an individual is in any of the given states. By having the appropriate transition matrix $P(t + 1)$ we are able to determine the probability distribution of the individual being in any of the states at time $t + 1$. In other words, we have the matrix equation $B(t + 1) = B(t) \cdot P(t + 1)$. The probability distribution at time $t + 2$ is similarly found;

$$B(t + 2) = B(t + 1) \cdot P(t + 1) = B(t) \cdot P(t + 1) \cdot P(t + 2)$$

Clearly by continuing in this way $B(t + n) = B(t) \cdot \prod_{l=1}^{n} P(t + l)$

and similarly $B(t) = B(0) \cdot \prod_{r=1}^{t} P(r)$.

If we specify a further condition that all the transition coefficients of $P(t)$ are constant through time, then $P(t) = P$ for all t. The vector transformations outlined for the Markov process become $B(t + 1) = B(t) \cdot P$, $B(t + 2) = B(t)P^2$, $B(t + n) = B(t) \cdot P^n$ and $B(t) = B(0)P^t$. This type of stochastic process is called a Markov chain. It is clear that the equation $B(t + 1) = B(t)P$ is the same as the fundamental matrix equation (as was the analogous equation for a discrete-time, discrete-space Markov process). Markov chains are the most used stochastic process in the study of social mobility. This is primarily because they are mathematically more tractable than other more general processes. Under certain conditions[14] a stage is reached where $B(t) = B(t) \cdot P$, and we have a stationary process. This means a stable equilibrium has been reached. When Markov chains have been used, either comparisons of the predictions over certain time periods with what was observed over the time period, or comparison of the equilibrium distribution with the observed distribution are made (see Prais, 1955).

Hodge (1966) used Markov chains to analyse inter-generational mobility data for three generations of men and intra-generational mobility data for a group of men over two consecutive time periods (for three time points). His categories were those of occupational status. Let the distribution of grandfather, fathers and sons be g, f and s respectively, and let the transition matrices for change from grandfather to father and for father to son be A and B respectively. In terms of our basic equation, we have $f = gA$ and $s = fB$. If the mobility process is adequately described as a Markov chain, then a hypothesis to test this is, $A = B$. From the two basic equations we have $s = fB = gAB$. Now we can construct the (observed) transition matrix for change from grandfathers to sons (grandsons). Let this matrix be C and we have another hypothesis to test, namely $AB = C$. However, this hypothesis can also be satisfied by probability processes other than Markov chains.[15] If we wanted a hypothesis that was satisfied by Markov chains then we would test the equation $A^2 = C$. However, statistical testing of these hypotheses is beyond the scope of this book. (They are discussed by Anderson (1954), Anderson and Goodman (1957) and by Goodman (1962).)

Hodge, by use of comparisons between actual and expected association of son's and grandfather's occupation inferred that 'grandfather's occupation does not have any appreciable *direct* effect upon a person's occupation beyond the *indirect* effect induced by its influence upon father's occupation'. There were discrepancies between the Markov chain predictions, but these were not large, and moreover were far smaller than the discrepancies due to a model of complete status inheritance. When he considered intragenerational mobility, Hodge found similar results. Again the Markov chain did not fit the data, but the performance of a model based upon status stability was worse. Hodge was concerned to demonstrate that the concepts of status inheritance and career were not of overriding importance, and could only apply to a small portion of the population.

However, this is far from accepting the utility of Markov chains. In a different context, namely mobility between industries, Blumen *et al.* (1955) had data on many successive time points (each interval being a quarter of a year). In discussing industrial mobility they found that the Markov chain seriously underestimates the number (or proportion) of workers who remain in a given industrial code group. (The perfect mobility hypothesis suffered from the same defect.) This defect of underestimating those remaining in each of the categories gets worse as larger numbers of time intervals are considered.

Clearly in each case we can, in principle, test the hypothesis of whether a Markov chain adequately describes the mobility process. Blumen *et al.* rejected this hypothesis but not the model in its entirety. They sought modifications of the model that would allow it to predict the observations. In order to discuss how such a modification could be made, it is as well to review the major assumptions involved with the use of Markov chains. The following are among the most significant:

(i) The population is closed. For intra-generational mobility no further individuals join the group of men being analysed and none die. For inter-generational mobility this means that at t_0 only fathers are in the work force studied, and that at t_1 only their sons are in the work force at that time.

(ii) For inter-generational mobility, each father is replaced by exactly one son.

(iii) The transition coefficients characterise everybody in the population.

(iv) The transition coefficients are constant through time.

(v) Mobility behaviour depends only upon current states and not on previous histories.

However necessary these assumptions are for mathematical purposes, it is clear that sociologically they do not stand much scrutiny. Consequently the remainder of this section is concerned with how these assumptions may be relaxed.

We start by considering assumption (iii). Given that a Markov chain badly under-predicts the numbers remaining in a category, there are grounds for considering some individuals more likely to remain immobile than others. Accordingly Blumen *et al.* divided the population into two groups; stayers and movers. The stayers remain (individually) in the categories they start in while the behaviour of the movers is characterised by a Markov chain. Let the mobility matrix be P, and let the proportion remaining in the ith category be s_i. We can construct the diagonal matrix S, where $s_{ii} = s_i$ for each i and then $(I - S)$ which is also a diagonal matrix. Let M be the mobility matrix for the movers. For the purposes of illustration, suppose that there are three categories and then (see Blumen *et al.*):

$$I - S = \begin{bmatrix} 1 - s_1 & 0 & 0 \\ 0 & 1 - s_2 & 0 \\ 0 & 0 & 1 - s_3 \end{bmatrix} \quad M = \begin{bmatrix} m_{11} & m_{12} & m_{13} \\ m_{21} & m_{12} & m_{23} \\ m_{31} & m_{32} & m_{32} \end{bmatrix}$$

In the first time interval the proportion of workers starting and finishing in the first category is $s_1 + (1 - s_1)m_{11}$. Similarly the proportion starting in the second category and ending up in the first is $(1 - s_2)m_{21}$. We can do this for each cell and arrive at:

$$P = \begin{bmatrix} s_1 + (1 - s_1)m_{11} & (1 - s_1)m_{12} & (1 - s_1)m_{13} \\ (1 - s_2)m_{21} & s_2 + (1 - s_2)m_{22} & (1 - s_2)m_{23} \\ (1 - s_3)m_{31} & (1 - s_3)m_{32} & s_3 + (1 - s_3)m_{33} \end{bmatrix}$$

or $P = S + (1 - S)M$.

If $P^{(n)}$ denotes the matrix of transitions after n time intervals, $P^{(n)} = S + (I - S)M^n$. This formulation provides a better fit with the data than a simple Markov chain, and the reader is referred to Blumen *et al.* (1955) where other ways of generalising their model are suggested.

Consider now assumption (v). It would seem that mobility is clearly a historical process and that previous history will have some effect upon mobility in any given time interval. This particular assumption can be modified in any number of ways. A basic axiom for the so-called Cornell mobility model (Mc-Ginnis, 1968) is added on sociological grounds: 'The probability of remaining in any state increases as a strict monotone function of duration of prior occupancy of that state.' This axiom, called the axiom of cumulative inertia, simultaneously deals with assumption (iii) as well as (v). McGinnis argues that it is a plausible hypothesis only if the system remains closed, and that 'the axiom is probably a bad one insofar as mobility is concerned in a hierarchy with an ordinary promotional system'. Hodge's conclusions would suggest that the assumption is not a bad one. Clearly more research is required to clarify this. Hodge and McGinnis could well be talking about different things (it is not clear what McGinnis means by his 'hierarchy'). Alternatively Hodge's results may be dependent upon the artefact created by assuming the system to be closed.

The axiom provided by McGinnis clearly leads to a generalisation of a simple Markov chain. There are two time parameters, one for time as we have been using it, and one for the duration of occupancy of a particular state by a unit. Let $S_i(d, t)$ denote occupancy of the ith category at time t for the dth successive time interval. The population can now be partitioned into four parts, each part experiencing different mobility in a particular time interval. Table 8.3 displays this.

Table 8.3

Residential status at t	Mobility status	
	Stayer	Mover
Continued occupancy	A) $S_i(d, t) \rightarrow S_i(d+1, t+1)$	B) $S_i(d, t) \rightarrow S_j(1, t+1)$
New occupancy	C) $S_i(1, t) \rightarrow S_i(2, t+1)$	D) $S_i(1, t) \rightarrow S_j(1, t+1)$

Adapted from McGinnis (1968) with permission of the ASA

McGinnis provides the necessary axioms for the generalised model and from them proves some theorems that display the algebraic structure of the model. The Cornell model is shown to converge to an equilibrium state and the stationary Markov chain is a degenerate case of the Cornell mobility model. In order to use the model it is necessary to specify a mathematical function $S(d)$ that has the properties of the cumulative inertia axiom, and this can be quite arbitrary. McGinnis reports simulation results using $S(d)$ as the matrix function, where $S(d) = S(d-1) + (1/a) I - S(d-1))$ where a is arbitrary. What this function expresses is that the probability of staying is increased by a fixed proportion of the remaining range $I - S(d)$. Clearly the smaller the value of a the quicker the system will converge. This model is clearly more complex than its predecessors and, as McGinnis states, more analytic and empirical research are needed before we can decide whether this model, or a modification of it, adequately describes certain mobility processes.

Finally we look at the first two assumptions ((i) and (ii)). In the context of migration, Rogers (1967) presents models of an open system by having a category corresponding to death by which individuals may leave the system and by having birth vectors (which can be added after each transition) so that new individuals can enter the system. We can clearly use analogous procedures for the study of social mobility, or use also some of the work of Matras (1960, 1961). The assumption that each father is replaced by one son in the labour force is clearly inadequate. Through differential fertility some fathers are replaced by more than one son, and some men of the fathers' generation are not replaced at all. Also there are fathers working alongside their sons in the labour force that corresponds to the son's generation. The assumption if one father one son just does not have any sociological justification. Clearly one response is to continue as before, simply because there are no other data available. Ultimately however, the only recourse is to use more sophisticated models (see for example, Bartholomew, 1968) and also to use different methods of data collection.

Matras (1961) suggests a model whereby differential fertility can be introduced explicitly. Let $a_0 = (a_1, \ldots a_k)$ be the vector of the adult's distribution into the k categories. We have $\sum_{i=1}^{k} a_i = 1$. Let R_i be the net reproduction rate of the ith category and R_0 the net reproduction rate of the total population. Clearly $R_0 = \sum_i a_i R_i$. Construct a diagonal matrix $D_F = [f_{ij}]$ where $f_{ij} = 0$ for $i \neq j$ and $f_{ii} = f_i = R_i/R_0$. Then the distribution by their father's occupations of the second generation birth *cohort* is given by:

$$a_0 D_F = \beta_0 = (b_1, b_2, \ldots b_k).$$

The occupational structure (or any other status structure) can change, and with it there is change in available opportunities. Let G_i be the relative growth of the ith category from t_0 to t_1. Then the ratio of growth of the ith category to that of the entire population is $g_i = G_i/G = G_i/R_0$ where $G = \Sigma_i a_i G_i = \Sigma_i a_i R_i = R_0$. The diagonal matrix $D_G = [g_{ij}]$ can then be constructed where $g_{ij} = 0$ for $i \neq j$ and $g_{ii} = g_i$ for each $i = 1, 2, \ldots k$. The occupational distribution one generation later is given by $a_0 D_G = a_1 = (C_1 \ldots C_k)$ with $\Sigma C_i = 1$ and $c_i = a_i g_i$. If the mobility matrix is M then $\beta_0 M = a_1$ and we have also $a_0 D_F M = a_0 D_G = a_1$. This model can easily be generalised (conceptually if not computationally) to the case of time-dependent transition matrices. Clearly we can ring the changes by holding any of these matrices fixed and by holding combinations of matrices fixed (see Matras (1961) for further details).

The value of the approach suggested by Matras lies in its attempt to come to grips with the problems encountered by dispensing with the first two assumptions needed in order to apply Markov chains. Ryder (1965) points out the need to study change through study of successive birth cohorts. The fundamental fact that birth cohorts do not correspond to generations undermines much of the work using straightforward mobility tables. As well as the models suggested by Matras, Duncan (1966) and Blau and Duncan (1967) have approached the problem by looking specifically at birth cohorts and analysing these. Blau and Duncan are innovative in a crucially important way by introducing explicit causal models in order to understand mobility as a social process.

It is clear that the conventional approach to the study of social mobility by means of the mobility table is analogous to a near worked out mine. It has been valuable in the past and has shed considerable light on the dynamics of inequality in an industrialised society. But by remaining in this tradition, focussing only on this particular approach, the field will stultify. However, new ways out of such an impasse are emerging. Matras and Goodman are each developing the analysis of mobility tables in a fruitful manner. McGinnis shows a way of completely generalising the model and, perhaps if the complications involved in differential fertility are considered in this generalisation also, such a model will be very fruitful. The use by Blau and Duncan of causal models must be followed up. The analysis of social mobility by means of the mobility tables has its roots in the problem of examining the differential opportunity for sons in different categories*. Blau and Duncan focus directly on the possible causal factors of this social inequality. Finally an effort has to be made to provide a mathematical framework for discussing social and geographical mobility in the same context. It is abundantly clear that conventional analysis of social mobility can be vivified by being transformed and should be one of the more exciting and fruitful fields of study.

---

* Since writing this chapter an article by McFarland presents an interesting counter argument to the approach of McGinnis:
D. D. McFarland, 'Intergenerational Social Mobility as a Markov process: including a Time-Stationary Markovian Model that explains observer declines in Mobilty Rates', *ASR*, June 1970, No. 3, 463-75.

9. On the Prospects of Mathematical Sociology

Is there a need for sociologists to concern themselves with mathematics? Such a question has been asked (and answered) repeatedly during the last three decades. In fact, the term sociology was, in part, coined in a reaction against the intrusion of mathematics[1] – and that was in the previous century. A related question asks whether or not there is, within sociology, a cultural resistance to mathematics. The objectives of sociology are seen differently and vary from sociologist to sociologist. It is not surprising therefore that these questions have been posed and answered in a variety of ways and, furthermore, there is still no consensus among sociologists concerning the use of mathematics. However, these questions serve as a stimulus to place the contents of the previous chapters in a broader perspective.

Among the accusations made against the use of mathematics in sociology is one alleging that, through its use, all the flavour of social life is lost. Furthermore, so the criticism runs, mathematics can only be used to study trivial problems. What is really at issue is the process of abstraction. The triviality of the complaint is transparent: it is impossible to study anything without first abstracting. If, as the story goes, Newton was inspired to his epoch making work by the fall of an apple, its colour was not significant. Whether it was red or green, ripe or unripe was immaterial (once it had started to fall). Abstraction is inevitable and furthermore it is desirable. If the motion of a car down a hill is treated as a problem of mechanics, its make and colour are irrelevant. Whether the car has leather upholstery, a cigarette lighter and defective headlights are equally irrelevant issues. If however, the responsibility for an accident was in question, the roadworthiness of the vehicle would be crucial. Manet's painting of an execution is not the same as a photograph of one, and both are different from an historical account of an execution and its political consequences. None is superior to the others in *all* respects. In analysing social phenomena we need to note regularities, and frequently this demands that features peculiar to a particular context are discarded. We select what is socially and sociologically relevant and this is no less true when mathematics is utilised. Its use may sharpen our perception and it may also dull it. In either case, the criteria for judgement are sociological. We turn now to the charge that mathematics can only be used to study trivia.

In terms of understanding social phenomena, mathematical sociology is no different to non-mathematical sociology. Moreover the distinction is a spurious one because in a very real sense, mathematical sociology does not exist. What distinguishes it from the remainder of sociology is the tools it uses, and in order to assess the merits or demerits of using these tools, both sociological *and* mathematical criteria have to be invoked.[2] Each problem is primarily sociological, and mathematics must be utilised with this understanding. Each case needs individual consideration. Both the rejection of the use of mathematics and the avowal of the mathematisation of all sociology are out of place.

With this said, we can turn to examine the mathematical approaches to sociological theory which are discussed in the text. This involves consideration of possible extensions and generalisations of particular techniques and locating them within a much wider use of mathematics within sociology.

9.1 Structure Reconsidered

Graph theory provides a simple, intuitive and readily comprehensible means of representing structure. Further, our definition of structure is precise and still sufficiently flexible for it to be used in a variety of distinct contexts. The use of graphs (signed and unsigned) is not a great step in the direction of abstraction, but it is a necessary[3] one for examining the relations between social objects and the structure of these relations. However, once this simple representation is made two advantages are gained. In the first place, the results within graph theory can be fruitfully used, and secondly, the manner in which generalisations can be made to other mathematical systems becomes clearer.

Valued graphs are a natural generalisation of non-valued graphs. Moreover, there is the sociological need to consider relations of varying intensity which can be dealt with (to some extent) by use of valued graphs. The work of Hubbell (1965) and Doreian (1969a, 1970) provide a limited start in this direction. Considerable work has been done in analysing flows through networks (Ford and Fulkerson, 1962) and this may prove useful to sociologists. There is also a need to consider graphs where the points have valuations. Hubbell's work makes a start here. The application of topology immediately suggests itself as a means of generalising graph theoretical models of structure. A beginning has been made in this direction and is briefly reported by Abell (1969).

The inclusion of valued graphs within balance theory is likely to remain difficult, and Flament's basic question[4] (Flament, 1963, p. 92) remains unanswered. Mathematically we can provide many answers, but there is (as yet) no sociological rationale for any of these. The major distinction between the use of unsigned graphs, as discussed in Chapter 4, and the use of signed graphs within balance theory, is that in the latter case the graphs are included in a sociological (or psychological) theory, whereas in the former, they provide a convenient descriptive device. One generalisation of balance theory (to clustering) stems from a redefinition of balance for the all negative triad. This generalisation is made quite independently of the values on the arcs. In demonstrating that structural balance can be used to derive a large number of sociological hypotheses, Davis (1963) also provides a limited treatment of values on the arcs of a signed graph.

Davis explicitly states that his hypotheses and deductions

apply under conditions of 'mechanical solidarity'. There is clearly a need to examine the consequences for the theory if this restriction is relaxed (and conditions of 'organic solidarity' are included), particularly as many of the hypotheses he derives were not initially formulated under this restriction. Much of the work of Berger *et al.* (1966)[5] deals with balance theory in the sense of structural balance and in terms of the multi-dimensional approach to stratification. Fararo (1969) provides a generalisation of balance in the latter by considering many states instead of two (balance and imbalance).

However, we are not restricted to graphs as a means of representing structure. As was suggested in Chapter 3 (and Appendix B) there are many algebras we can choose if they are appropriate. White (1963) provides an example where (algebraic) group theory can be used. He started from a set of axioms for certain prescriptive marriage systems first laid down by Kemeny *et al.*[6] The individuals in such a system are split into disjoint segments such that, for each segment, the men can take their wives from one and only one (distinct) segment and their children belong to one and only one (distinct) segment. The rules specifying these two relations can be represented respectively by the permutation matrices W and C. A particular product of these matrices gives the marriage relation M. An initial typology of kinship systems is obtained by examining permitted marriages.[7] For example in Figure 9.1(a) matrilateral cross-cousins can marry and this is represented by $M = C^{-1}WC$.

If patrilateral cross-cousins may marry (Figure 9.1(b)) then $M = C^{-1}W^{-1}C$. But $W = M$, and for the matrilateral cross-cousin marriage $WC = CW$, and for patrilateral cross-cousin marriage $CW = W^{-1}C$. If both types of marriage are permitted simultaneously,[8] then $W^2 = I$. The basic typology of kinship systems has five categories: bilateral marriage ($W^2 = I$ and $WC = CW$), matrilateral marriage ($WC = CW$ but $W^2 \neq I$), patrilateral marriage ($W^{-1}C = CW$ but $W^2 \neq I$), paired segments marriage ($W^2 = CW$ but $WC \neq CW$) and a residual category. (Adapted from White (1963) by permission.)

Now for a given system, the two matrices W and C generate a group. The size of this (algebraic) group depends on the power of W and C and the relation between these generators.[9] Each distinct type of society (with respect to marriage and kinship identity) is characterised by a distinct algebraic group, and is classified according to this group. This classification is an elegant one.[10]

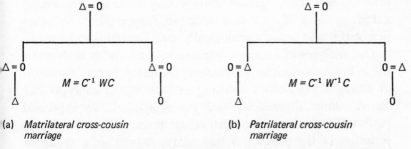

(a) *Matrilateral cross-cousin marriage*   (b) *Patrilateral cross-cousin marriage*

Figure 9.1 (a) Matrilateral cross-cousin marriage (b) Patrilateral cross-cousin marriage (Reproduced from White (1963) with the permission of Prentice-Hall Inc.)

However, this is the only use made of the algebra of groups. In particular, there is no attempt to compare kinship structures directly. Boyd (1969) provides an alternative formulation using the permutation matrices F and M where F represents the fatherhood relation and M the motherhood relation.[11] (The relation between these and the permutation matrices used by White are $F = C^{-1}$ and $M = C^{-1}W$.) Boyd makes use of homomorphisms of groups in order to study the evolution of kinship systems and terminology.[12] Further, Boyd gives the conditions under which groups are the appropriate analytical tools, and as a special case obtains the structure theorem[13] of balance theory. His paper should prove to be very important as it also embraces the analysis of kinship grammars in terms of the work of Loundsbury (1964) and (indirectly) Chomsky (1963). (The algebra involved is somewhat advanced and well beyond the scope of this book.)

In Chapter 4, the rudiments of a fairly elaborate model for the analysis of structure were stated. However, little use has been made of them throughout the book. This is primarily because simpler notions of structure, and corresponding analyses, are all that have been pursued in the literature. This general model of structure provides a natural way of analysing particular structures in relation to each other. Undoubtedly the concept of a homomorphism will be of considerable value in this context also. Algebraically, group theory may be used. The set of automorphisms of a set, or a structure, form a group. Whether or not this will prove sociologically useful remains to be seen.

The analyses of formal organisations and status both make use of homomorphisms, particularly the latter. Fararo's analysis of status is especially promising as sociological concepts like status, status dimensions and status symbol are expressed (without distortion) in mathematical terms. Moreover, a description of the process of how status 'works' in a group or community is given. The mathematical treatment of diffuse status dimensions should prove useful, not only for analysing status, but also for the study of stereotyping and the process of social labelling.

It should be noted that our use of structure makes it possible to analyse both objective and subjective structures. The use of mathematics in this instance is not dependent upon the exclusion of the terms in which social actors understand their own action and the action of others. On the contrary, it facilitates the inclusion of these terms in our analyses.

When we consider social mobility, it is clear that mathematics has proved particularly useful. This is true not only of traditional analyses of mobility, but also of more recent analyses. Blau and Duncan (1967) take the traditional analysis of the mobility table as far as it can go and thereby demonstrate how limited it really is. It is significant that the most penetrating criticisms of this type of analysis are based upon mathematical considerations (see Duncan, 1966b). Moreover, some of the alternative strategies that are suggested also use mathematics. See, for example,

Duncan (1961) for a socio-economic index constructed by regression techniques.

A rapidly growing field is the application of mathematics through the use of stochastic processes. Because these models are based on probability theory, we were unable to consider them in any detail. However, good introductions are provided by Rogers (1968) and Keyfitz (1968) in the area of demography. In a general context, Bartholomew (1968) also provides an extensive introduction. Finally the use of causal analysis, in the form of causal models, has been introduced into the study of mobility. It is fitting, therefore, that Blau and Duncan are also innovative with respect to the use of causal models. Both stochastic processes and causal analysis should prove very useful in studying social and geographical mobility.

9.2 Sociological Hypotheses and Theories[14]

One of the campaigns long waged by Coleman is the necessity of going beyond establishing the existence of relationships to establishing the form of these relationships. The major reason why sociologists have been loth (or unable) to do this, is the extensive use of categorical data and measures of association appropriate to these. Sociologists have spent a long time learning to live with weak measurements and 'inadequate' data (at or below the ordinal level of measurement).[15] Part of this adaptation has resulted in the creation of ingenious measures of association (see particularly Goodman and Kruskal (1954, 1959, 1963), Kruskal (1963) and Kendall (1955)) and more generally, of 'non-parametric' statistics (see Blalock (1960), Seigal (1956)). Partially as a result of this there is now an extensive debate regarding the best use of statistical notions. On the one hand there is the argument that social reality, being what it is, precludes the use of higher levels of measurement. Such measurement procedures would distort the data. On the other hand, it is argued that the expediency of 'parametric' statistical techniques justifies the use of higher level measurement procedures. Moreover, it is not reality, but our conception of it, that imposes itself.

Distortion of the data then results from the use of lower levels of measurement. Only in cases where the categories are sociologically meaningful and unavoidable is the use of low levels of measurement appropriate.

Most sociological hypotheses are of the form 'the more A the more B' or 'the variables A and B are associated'. One attempt to go beyond this for theoretical relations is that of Simon (1957). He attempted to cast Homans's propositions relating sentiment, frequency of interaction and agreement (or mutual activities) within a small group into partial differential equations. Stinchcombe and Harris (1969) have recently attempted a similar analysis in the context of stratification within an organisation. These have not been particularly successful (and are beyond the scope of this book anyway). However, as a heuristic device, attempts have been made to cast hypothesis in a simpler mathematical form.

For example, Willer (1967) considers Durkheim's classical work on suicide. Egoistic suicide varies inversely with the extent of social integration. We could write this as $S = b/I + a$ where I and S denote respectively, social integration and the suicide rate of a given society or community.[16] Similarly the hypothesis that altruistic suicide varies directly with social integration may be represented by $S_1 = bI$. Now all the variables of Durkheim's theory can be included in similar relationships and the set of equations manipulated mathematically in order to examine their behaviour.

We are not restricted to considering variables in pairs. Barton and Anderson (1969) treat an analysis of the change of administration in a prison in a similar fashion. As an example, the equation $D = b_1H - b_2P$ relates the variable 'prisoner disorder' (D) to the hostility of prisoners (H) and 'the power exercised over them by an inmate elite' (P). A system of equations is set up that can be heuristically manipulated. Such equations are linear and involve three variables. Clearly we can include as many variables as we like and the equations do not have to be linear.[17]

Is there any point in considering this approach to theory construction further? If mathematical models can do no more than this, as Cuzzort (1969) suggests, then the answer is probably no. Of course this approach can be rejected as being obviously trivial because 'life is more complex than that'. Such a perspective is even more narrow than the literal acceptance of such simple equations. It is also destructive as it stops dead the exploration of an idea. Another response is to accept the idea in principle, but to ask for the evidence as well. The onus is now on the sociologist, as a model builder, to determine these equations if they exist. Rather than determine that a relation between two or more variables does exist and then dress it up in a convenient mathematical form, we are invited to set about determining what the relation is. This is much more demanding.

Zetterberg (1963) suggests the use of axiomatised social theory. Certain sociological hypotheses are used as axioms and other propositions are derived from them. If we look at mathematics, which makes the greatest use of axiomatics, the pursuit of a set of axioms is as much an aesthetic exercise as it is a mathematical one. It is of no great importance if there is more than one set of appropriate axioms. If one axiom can be shown to be dependent on the remainder no harm is done. It is simply redundant as an axiom and reappears as a theorem derived from the axioms. If, however, a contradiction can be derived from a set of axioms, or within a set of propositions, then something is radically wrong.

Axiomatised social theory is not inherently superior to social theory that is not axiomatised. Thus while Simon was able to show that one of Homans's propositions could be derived from the others, no significant theoretical advance was involved. If he had found contradictions with Homans' theory or propositions that were not already there, a theoretical advance would have been made. This was precisely the objective that Zetterberg had in mind when advocating the use of axioms. By systematically deriving hypotheses from axioms, it is more likely that (i) unexpected hypotheses will be derived and (ii) contradictions in a theory will be more readily detected. There is also a practical advantage in using such a system as we need only test the propositions that have been *properly derived* from the axioms. A failure to make sure that the derivation of propositions is correct has led many theorists into considerable error (see for example, Hage, 1965).

The type of derivation commonly used is the following: 'The greater *A* the greater *B*' and 'the greater *B* the greater *C*' together imply 'the greater *A* the greater *C*'. The relation between the variables in each pair is generally indicated by a measure of association (for categorical data) or a correlation (for interval level data). However, while logical deduction is transitive, correlation is not, and the process of deduction that was outlined above is not always valid. In fact, in actual usage, it has been invalid more often than not. A seminal and sorely needed contribution came from Costner and Leik (1964) who specified the conditions under which this type of reasoning is valid and the conditions under which it is not.

Both Zetterberg's suggestion for the axiomatisation of social theory and the challenge to determine the forms of the relations between sociological variables lead us directly to the realm of model building. This, however, is complicated, and it would be more of a hindrance than a help to give a superficial account.[18] There are many technical problems that have to be dealt with before sociologists can legitimately make inferences with confidence. Econometricians have been familiar with these problems for some time. In a series of stimulating papers, Blalock introduces these problems into the sociological literature. Blalock (1964, 1969) provides a sound basis for causal analysis, and his papers together with the first part of Johnston (1963) provide an excellent introduction to the types of problems that sociologists can no longer blithely ignore.[19] Unless these problems are taken up seriously by sociologists, the discipline will remain severely handicapped.

9.3 Concluding Remarks
It is clear that the reader who wants to take mathematical

sociology seriously has a wealth of literature to refer to. Equally clear is the need to master certain parts of mathematics notably probability theory, statistics and modern algebra. Due to the limitations imposed upon an introductory book, these are scarcely touched upon here. However, a study of mathematics can be exciting and interesting in its own right. This book will have achieved its object if the reader feels sufficient sociological motivation to undertake such a study. The future of sociology as a viable discipline will largely depend on the use of mathematics in an informed and imaginative manner.

F

Appendix A
The Algebra of Sets

Identities that are satisfied by the operations of union, intersection and complementation were mentioned in Chapter 2. A further list of these identities is given in Table A.1. The algebra of sets is simply the collection of theorems that follow from them.

Table A.1: Identities for the Algebra of Sets

1. Closure Laws	If A, B belong to the algebra, then $A \cup B$ and $A \cap B$ also belong
2. Idempotent Laws	$A \cup A = A$ $A \cap A = A$
3. Associative Laws	$(A \cup B) \cup C = A \cup (B \cup C)$ $(A \cap B) \cap C = A \cap (B \cap C)$
4. Commutative Laws	$A \cup B = B \cup A$ $A \cap B = B \cap A$
5. Distributive Laws	$A \cup (B \cap C) = (A \cup B) \cap (A \cup C)$ $A \cap (B \cup C) = (A \cap B) \cup (A \cap C)$
6. Identity Laws	$A \cup \phi = A$ $A \cap U = A$ $A \cup U = U$ $A \cap \phi = \phi$
7. Complement Laws	$A \cup A' = U$ $A \cap A' = \phi$ $(A')' = A, U' = \phi, \phi' = U$
8. De Morgan's Laws	$(A \cup B)' = A' \cap B'$ $(A \cap B)' = A' \cup B'$

An intuitive way to check these identities is to draw Venn diagrams. Alternatively, we could reason about the elements of these sets and establish that for each equality, the sets (on each side of the equality sign) are made up of the same elements.

This simply verbalises the corresponding Venn diagrams. However, the algebra of sets can be established without reference to sets and their elements.

In order to do this we need the idea of a *binary operation*, which is a special kind of mapping. A binary operation, o, on a set A is a mapping from $A \times A$ to A. (A binary operation can also be defined as a mapping from $A \times B$ to C for distinct sets A, B and C, although we are only concerned here with defining binary operations for one set.) A typical element of a binary operation is $\langle \langle a_1, a_2 \rangle, a_3 \rangle$ which states that the element $\langle a_1, a_2 \rangle$ is mapped to a_3. This is usually written as $a_1 \, o \, a_2 = a_3$ when a_1, a_2 and $a_3 \in A$. It is immediately clear that for the subsets of a set, the operations of union and intersection are binary operations.

We could simply state that there are two binary operations, $\cup$ and $\cap$, which satisfy the identities in Table A.1. The properties of $\cup$ and $\cap$ are given solely by the relations in the table, and theorems deduced from these identities do not depend (in the proof) upon a particular representation. For example, suppose we wish to prove $(A \cup B) \cap (A \cup B') = A$. We could prove this as follows.

$A \cup (B \cap B') = (A \cup B) \cap (A \cup B')$	by a distributive law
$B \cap B' = \phi$	by a complement law
$\therefore (A \cup B) \cap (A \cup B') = A \cup \phi$	by substitution
$A \cup \phi = A$	by an identity law
$\therefore (A \cup B) \cap (A \cup B') = A$	by substitution

In fact we do not need all of the identities in Table A.1, to create the algebra of sets. If we assume the following for two binary operations, $\cup$ and $\cap$;

(i) the commutative laws,
(ii) the distributive laws,
(iii) the existence of $\cup$ and ϕ such that $A \cup \phi = A$ and $A \cap U = A$,
(iv) the existence of A' for each A such that $A \cup A' = U$ and $A \cap A' = \phi$,

(v) if $A = B$, then (a) $A' = B'$, (b) $A \cup C = B \cup C$ and (c) $A \cap C = B \cap C$ for any C,

(vi) equality is a transitive relation,

then we can prove the remaining identities in Table A.1 (see Goodstein, 1963).

If we interchange $\cup$ and $\cap$ and also ϕ and U in any statement about sets we obtain the *dual* statement of the original one. For example, the dual of the distributive law $A \cup (B \cap C) = (A \cup B) \cap (A \cup C)$ is the other distributive law $A \cap (B \cup C) = (A \cap B) \cup (A \cap C)$. The dual of $A \cup U = U$ is $A \cap \phi = \phi$. The principle of duality states that if a set of axioms imply their own duals, then any dual of a theorem deduced from the axioms is also a theorem that can be deduced from the axioms. Suppose we wish to prove the dual of our earlier example, $(A \cap B) \cup (A \cap B') = A$ the steps would be:

$A \cap (B \cup B') = (A \cap B) \cup (A \cup B')$	distributive law
$B \cup B' = U$	complement law
$\therefore (A \cap B) \cup (A \cap B') = A \cap U$	substitution
$A \cap U = A$	identity law
$\therefore (A \cup B) \cap (A \cup B') = A$	substitution

It is clear that each step of this proof is the dual of the corresponding statement in the earlier proof. (Our assumptions from which the identities of Table A.1 are deduced form a self-dual set of identities.)

In Chapter 2, a partial order relation on a set A was defined as a reflexive, anti-symmetric and transitive relation. If, in addition to this, for each pair of elements $a, b \in A$, either $a \, R \, b$ or $b \, R \, a$ (or both) the relation would be a *complete order relation*. All the subsets of a set (i.e. the power set) form a partial order for set inclusion, and all the natural numbers form a complete order for 'less than'. Partially ordered sets with only a finite number of elements can be represented by a diagram where the lines represent the order relation. Figure A.1 shows two such partial orders. In Figure A.1(a) the element a is the greatest element, the elements d, e and f are minimal elements and there is no least element. The partial order shown in Figure A.1(b) is the power set of the finite set $\{a, b, c\}$. The (unique) maximal element is $\{a, b, c\}$ and the unique minimal element is ϕ.

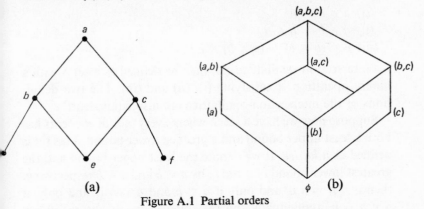

Figure A.1 Partial orders

Chapter 6 contains definitions of upper and lower bounds, and least upper and greatest lower bounds. The maximal, greatest, minimal and least elements were defined also. We add to these the definition of an atom; elements that contain only themselves and the least element are atoms. In Figure A.1(b), $\{a\}$, $\{b\}$ and $\{c\}$ are atoms. In Chapter 6, a union-semilattice was defined as a partially ordered set S, where each pair of elements had a least upper bound. If we denote the least upper bound of a and b by $a \vee b$, then $a \subseteq b$ if and only if $a \vee b = b$. It is straightforward to prove:

(i) $a \vee a = a$

(ii) $a \vee b = b \vee a$

and

(iii) $a \vee (b \vee c) = (a \vee b) \vee c$.

In fact, we can proceed in the opposite direction and define a union-semilattice as a set S, with a single binary operation $\vee$, satisfying (i), (ii) and (iii) as axioms. Defining an order relation, c, by $a \subseteq b$ if and only if $a \vee b = b$, we can prove that the order is a partial order and that each pair of elements in S has a least upper bound.

Similarly, if we denote $a \subseteq b$ if and only if $a \wedge b = a$ for an intersection-semilattice (where $a \wedge b$ is the greatest lower bound of a and b) we have

(i) $a \wedge a = a$
(ii) $a \wedge b = b \wedge a$
(iii) $a \wedge (b \wedge c) = (a \wedge b) \wedge c$

An intersection-semilattice can then be defined as a set S with a binary operation $\wedge$ satisfying (i), (ii) and (iii). The two definitions of the intersection-semilattice are also equivalent.

Suppose now we have a set S, where every pair of elements has both a least upper bound and a greatest lower bound. This set is defined as a *lattice*. If we denote the least upper bound and the greatest lower bound of a and b, by $a \vee b$ and $a \wedge b$ respectively, then $a \wedge b = a$ if and only if $a \subseteq b$ and $a \subseteq b$ if and only if $a \vee b = b$. Individually the two binary operations satisfy an idempotent law, a commutative law and an associative law (above). The following two identities called the absorption laws are also satisfied:

$$a \wedge (a \vee b) = a \qquad a \vee (a \wedge b) = a$$

(Note that the two idempotent laws can be deduced from the absorption laws.) As in the cases of the two semilattices, we have two equivalent definitions of a lattice. Each lattice is both a union-semilattice and an intersection-semilattice.

A *congruence relation* on a semilattice is an equivalence relation R defined on that semilattice S such that if a and b belong to the same equivalence class ($a\,R\,b$), then $(a \vee c)$ and $(b \vee c)$ belong to the same equivalence class $((a \vee c)\,R\,(b \vee c))$ for all c in S.

If a lattice also satisfies the two distributive laws, $a \wedge (b \vee c) = (a \wedge b) \vee (a \wedge c)$ and $a \vee (b \wedge c) = (a \vee b) \wedge (a \vee c)$, it is called a *distributive lattice*. In a distributive lattice, the two equations $a \wedge b = a \wedge c$ and $a \vee b = a \vee c$ imply that $a = b$. If a lattice has elements 0 and 1 (corresponding to ϕ and U) such that $0 \subseteq a$ for all $a \in A$ and $a \subseteq 1$ for all $a \in A$, it is a *lattice with zero and unit*. If in such a lattice, there is for every element a complement a' such that $a \vee a' = 1$ and $a \wedge a' = 0$, then the lattice is said to be a *complemented lattice*. Finally a complemented distributive lattice is a *Boolean Algebra*. The (inclusion) relation for these types of algebras is shown in Figure A.2.

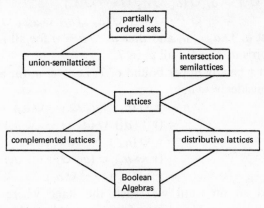

Figure A.2

THEOREMS FOR UNION-SEMILATTICES

1. Every finite union-semilattice has a greatest element.

Proof:
Let the semilattice be S and consist of $s_1, \ldots, s_n$. Define $t_1 = s_1$ and $t_k = s_k$ if $s_k > t_{k-1}$ and t_{k-1} otherwise. Thus t_n will be maximal. If t_n and t_m are both maximal, their least upper bound must belong to S. But there is no $s \in S$ such that $s > t_n$ or $s > t_m$. If $t_m = t_n$, then t_n is not maximal, and conversely. Therefore, $t_n = t_m$ and is the greatest element.

Definition:
A union-semilattice is *complete* if every subset has a least upper bound.

2. A finite union-semilattice is complete.

Proof:
Let $a_1, a_2, \ldots a_n$ be any subset T of a finite union-semilattice S. We require to prove that (i) an upper bound exists for T and (ii) there is a least upper bound of T.

(i) Let a denote $\bigcup\limits_{i=1}^{n} a_i$ (which is always defined in a union-semilattice). Consider any $a_i \in T$;

$$a_i \cup a = a_i \cup (a_1 \cup a_2 \cup \cdots \cup a_n)$$
$$= a_i \cup \cdots \cup a_{i-1} \cup (a_i \cup a_i) \cup a_{i+1} \cup \cdots \cup a_n.$$

But $a_i \cup a_i = a_i$ and thus $a_i \cup a = a$ for all i. In other words $a_i \subseteq a$ for all a_i in T.

(ii) Let v be any upper bound of T, i.e. $v \supseteq a_i$ for all a_i in T. Consider $v \cup a$,

$$v \cup a = v \cup (a_1 \cup a_2 \cup \cdots \cup a_n)$$
$$= (v \cup a_1) \cup (a_2 \cup \cdots \cup a_n)$$
$$= v \cup (a_2 \cup \cdots \cup a_n)$$
$$= (v \cup a_2) \cup (a_3 \cup \cdots \cup a_n)$$
$$= v \cup (a_3 \cup \cdots \cup a_n)$$

and so on until we reach the stage where $v \cup a = v \cup a_n = v$. Thus $a \subseteq v$ for all upper bounds v_m and a is the least upper bound of T.

Both congruence relation and ideal were defined in Chapter 6.

3. If I is an ideal of a union-semilattice S, then the equivalence relation defined by $a = b \pmod{I}$ when $a \vee j = b \vee j$ for some $j \in I$ is a congruence relation.

Proof:

Let $a \vee j = b \vee j$ and $c \in S$

then $(a \vee c) \vee j = c \vee (a \vee j)$
$$= c \vee (b \vee j)$$
$$= (b \vee c) \vee j$$

Thus the relation is a congruence relation.

Appendix B
Elements of Abstract Algebra

This appendix is included simply to indicate differences between various algebras. If we consider numbers, we have the real numbers, the rational numbers, the integers and the positive integers (natural numbers). From these we can construct the complex numbers $a + ib$ where $i^2 = -1$, and the a, b are drawn from the real numbers, or from the rational numbers, or from the integers, or from the natural numbers. Some of the number system and their relation to each other are shown in Figure B.1.

While we can add and multiply numbers we have to be careful over what we take number to mean. Further, it is helpful to

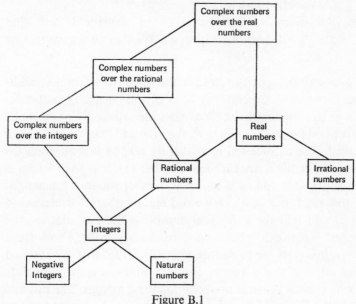

Figure B.1

regard the various number systems as special cases of particular algebras. If we consider addition of numbers for the moment, we are not interested in writing out all the possible additions. Apart from there being too many of them for us to be able to do this, conceptually it would be moving in the wrong direction. We are interested in presenting a set of rules for *all* additions. Let S be any set and let $+$ be a binary operation defined over that set which satisfies the following identities (given that 'equals' is a reflexive, symmetric and transitive relation on $S \times S$):

1. For all elements $a, b \in S$, the element $a + b \in S$ (Closure).
2. For every $a, b, c, d \in S$ if $a = c$ and $b = d$ then $a + d = c + d$ (Uniqueness).
3. There exists an element $o \in S$ such that $a + o = a$ for every $a \in S$ (Additive Identity element).
4. For every a and b in S, $a + b = b + a$ (Commutative Law).
5. For every a, b and c in S, $a + (b + c) = (a + b) + c$ (Associative Law).
6. For every $a \in S$ there exists an element b such that $a + b = 0$ (Additive Inverse). We denote the inverse by $-a$.

These axioms specify rules for the binary operation of addition. However it depends on what S and $+$ are in particular cases as to whether or not these rules are satisfied. For example, if S is the set of real numbers R, then the addition axioms are all satisfied. The axioms tell us that if we add to real numbers together the result is another real number (1), that such a sum is unique (2), that adding 0 to a real number leaves it unchanged (3), that the order in which we add real numbers is irrelevant (4 and 5) and that for every real number a there is another real number $-a$ which when added to a gives 0 (6). From these axioms it is possible to deduce many identities that are satisfied by addition of real numbers. But real numbers are not the only set with a binary operation satisfying these axioms. The rational numbers, which form a subset of the real numbers, also have an addition satisfying these axioms, but if we examine the set of positive integers together with 0, it is clear that axiom 6 is not satisfied. There is no additive inverse for this set when the usual arithmetic addition is being considered. Further if we have only the set of positive integers, then with the usual addition, axiom 3 as well as axiom 6 will not be satisfied.

We can specify another binary operation, $\cdot$, for the set S which we call 'multiplication'. We assume S and the relation 'equals' are as before and specify the following:

7. If a, $b \in S$ then $ab \in S$ (Closure). (We write ab for $a \cdot b$).
8. For every a, b, c, $d \in S$ if $a = c$ and $b = d$ then $ab = cd$ (Uniqueness).
9. There exists an element $1 \in S$ such that for all $a \in S$ $(a1) = a$ (Multiplicative Identity element).
10. For every a, $b \in S$ $ab = ba$ (Commutative law).
11. For every a, b, $c \in S$, $a(bc) = (ab)c$ (Associative Law).
12. For every a, b, $c \in S$, (i) $a(b + c) = ab + bc$ and (ii) $(b + c)a = ba + ca$ (Distributive Laws).
13. For every a, b, $c \in S$, if $C \neq 0$ then $ca = cb$ if and only if $a = b$ (Cancellation Law).
14. For every $a \in S$ there exists an element $b \in S$ such that $ab = 1$ (Multiplication Inverse). The inverse of a is denoted by $1/a$ or a^{-1}.

We note that axiom 14 is a stronger axiom than axiom 13 in the sense that 14 implies 13 but not the reverse. We can consider these axioms as defining two binary operations for a set S, and their properties are contained in the axioms, not in a particular interpretation of the axioms. By systematically selecting certain axioms we can construct distinct algebras.

If we assume axioms 1–12 and 14 we are dealing with an algebra with two binary operations which satisfy these axioms. Such an algebra is called a *field*. The set of real numbers and the set of rational numbers both are fields if we use the usual addition and multiplication. If a field F has a subset G of elements that also form a field for the same binary operations as F, then *G* is called a subfield of *F*. Clearly the rational numbers are a subfield of the real numbers. The set of complex numbers $a + ib$ form a field where a and b are real numbers, as do complex numbers with coefficients from the rational numbers.

If we assume axioms 1–13 (where instead of the existence of multiplicative inverses we have the cancellation law) then we are talking of an *integral domain*. Clearly any field satisfies the axioms for an integral domain, as the field axioms contain those for an integral domain. The integers, however, again under the usual addition and multiplication, form an integral domain but they do not form a field. For example, if we had the integer 4, the multiplicative inverse of this number in the set of rational numbers is $\frac{1}{4}$. Now $\frac{1}{4}$ is not an integer and there is no integer that can be a multiplicative inverse of 4. Complex numbers with coefficients taken from the integers also form a field.

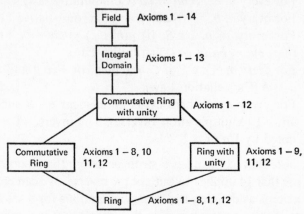

Figure B.2 Algebras with two binary operations

A *ring* is an algebra with two binary operations that satisfy axioms 1–8, 11 and 12. This means that in general, in a ring, the binary operation we call 'multiplication' is not commutative, there is no multiplicative identity element and of course the cancellation law is not satisfied. The set of matrices of a given order (see Appendix C) with entries from the even integers form a ring. A *commutative ring* is a ring where axiom 10 is also satisfied. The set of even integers with the usual addition and multiplication form a commutative ring. A *ring with unity* is a ring where axiom 9 is also satisfied. The set of matrices of a given order with entries from the real numbers form a ring with unity. Finally, a *commutative ring with unity* is a ring where axioms 9 and 10 are also satisfied. Each of these algebras are rich in their own right and their properties have been extensively explored. The relation between these algebras (in terms of the axioms satisfied) is diagrammatically represented in Figure B.2.

We turn now to briefly mention an algebra with a single binary operation. For the moment this binary operation is denoted by o. A group is a set G of elements with a binary operation satisfying the following four axioms:

(i) If $a, b \in G$ then $a \circ b \in G$ (Closure).
(ii) $a \circ (b \circ c) = (a \circ b) \circ c$ (Associativity).
(iii) There exists an element $e \in G$ such that for each $a \in G$, $ae = ea = a$ (Identity element).
(iv) For each $a \in G$, there exists an inverse b such that $ab = ba = e$.

Now it is clear that if we labelled the binary operation by $+$, a group satisfies axioms 1, 3, 5 and 6 and if we labelled the binary operation by $\cdot$, a group satisfies axioms 7, 9, 11, 14. Generally the group operation is taken as multiplicative and ab is referred to the product of a and b. A special kind of group is the commutative group which, as its name suggests, is a group that satisfies the commutative axiom. In the multiplicative notation, axiom 8 is satisfied and in the additive notation, axiom 4 is satisfied for commutative groups. A widely used notation is to represent commutative groups as having an additive binary operator. The set of integers together with zero form a commutative group for addition. A field can be thought of as a commutative group under $+$ and, excluding o, as a commutative group for multiplication. For a further discussion of groups see Grossman and Magnus (1964), who consider interesting examples of groups where the elements do not belong to the real numbers.

Appendix C
Elements of Matrix Algebra

A *vector* is simply an ordered collection of elements. The elements can be drawn for any single algebra. (For example, any of those algebras discussed in Appendix B, subject to certain requirements discussed below.) Usually they are taken from the real numbers, and we shall assume from now that elements that appear in the vector come from a field. Examples of vectors are (a, b, d, f) and $(5, 7, 4)$. The individual elements of a vector are called components. In the multi-dimensional stratification theories, a person's position is given by a set of ranks, one for each dimension, and these ranks can be written as a vector.

A *matrix* is a rectangular array of numbers written in rows and columns as in:

$$A = \begin{bmatrix} a_{11} & a_{12} \ldots a_{1n} \\ a_{21} & a_{22} \ldots a_{2n} \\ a_{m1} & a_{m2} \ldots a_{mn} \end{bmatrix}$$

The matrix A has m rows and n columns and such matrices are described as $(m \times n)$ matrices or as matrices of order $(m \times n)$. If we had n rank dimensions and m persons with rank profiles, then if each person corresponds to a row, all rank profiles can be written out as a matrix. The elements in the first column are then all the scores on the first dimension and similarly for the remaining columns. This use of a matrix is simply a means of writing data (see in particular Galtung's data matrix which is used as a central notion to unify ideas of theory and research, Galtung (1967)). However, we are able to define an algebra for matrices and matrix algebra is useful in mobility analysis, (Chapter 8) graph theoretical analyses of structure (Chapter 4), and simultaneous equation models.

The matrix A can be written $A = [a_{ij}]$ where a_{ij} denotes the entry in the ith row and the jth column. A matrix of size $(1 \times n)$ is called a *row vector* and a matrix of size $(m \times 1)$ is called a *column vector*. We also have the following definitions.

EQUALITY OF MATRICES

Two matrices A and B are said to be equal when they are of the same size and $a_{ij} = b_{ij}$ for all i, j.

ADDITION OF MATRICES

If two matrices A and B are of the same size then we can define $A + B$ to be a matrix C, where $c_{ij} = a_{ij} + b_{ij}$ for all i, j. We also need the assumption that the addition is a meaningful binary operation for the elements of the matrices. (When they belong to a field, addition is meaningful.) If $A = \begin{bmatrix} 1 & 2 \\ 4 & 3 \end{bmatrix}$ and $B = \begin{bmatrix} 2 & 3 \\ 4 & 2 \end{bmatrix}$ then $C = A + B = \begin{bmatrix} 3 & 5 \\ 8 & 5 \end{bmatrix}$.

SCALAR MULTIPLICATION

If k is an element such that multiplication of the a_{ij} by k is meaningful, then $kA = [ka_{ij}]$. For example, if $k = 2$ and $A = \begin{bmatrix} 1 & 2 \\ 4 & 3 \end{bmatrix}$ then $kA = \begin{bmatrix} 2 & 4 \\ 8 & 6 \end{bmatrix}$. In particular if $k = -1$, then $A - B = [a_{ij} - b_{ij}]$ by the rules of scalar multiplication and addition.

ELEMENTWISE MATRIX MULTIPLICATION

We shall define two distinct ways of multiplying matrices. Elementwise multiplication is the simplest of these. If A and B are matrices then $A \times B = [a_{ij} . b_{ij}]$. For the two matrices A and B defined above, $A \times B = \begin{bmatrix} 2 & 6 \\ 16 & 6 \end{bmatrix}$.

MATRIX MULTIPLICATION

If A is a matrix of order $(m \times n)$ and B is a matrix of order

$(n \times p)$ then the product of these two matrices AB is a matrix C of order $(m \times p)$ where

$$c_i = \sum_{k=1}^{n} a_{ik}b_{kj}$$

In order to multiply two matrices they have to be conformable, that is, the number of elements in any row of the first matrix must equal the number of elements in any column of the second matrix. To obtain c_{ij}, take the ith row of A and the jth column of B, multiply corresponding pairs of elements and add the n products. For example let

$$A = \begin{bmatrix} a_{11} & a_{12} & a_{13} \\ a_{21} & a_{22} & a_{23} \end{bmatrix} \quad \text{and} \quad B = \begin{bmatrix} b_{11} & b_{12} \\ b_{21} & b_{22} \\ b_{31} & b_{32} \end{bmatrix}$$

then

$$AB = \begin{bmatrix} a_{11}b_{11} + a_{12}b_{21} + a_{13}b_{31} & a_{11}b_{12} + a_{12}b_{22} + a_{13}b_{32} \\ a_{21}b_{11} & a_{22}b_{21} & a_{23}b_{31} & a_{21}b_{12} & a_{22}b_{22} & a_{23}b_{32} \end{bmatrix}$$

Note that the A and B are also conformable for the matrix product BA, but except for square matrices (which have the same number of rows and columns) this is not generally the case. For square matrices we can multiply a matrix A by itself to obtain A^2, and repeating this n times we have A^n.

The matrix multiplication of particular importance is that of a matrix with a vector. Consider the set of linear equations

$$a_{11}x_1 + a_{12}x_2 + \cdots a_{1n}x_n = y_1$$
$$a_{21}x_1 + a_{22}x_2 + \cdots a_{2n}x_n = y_{22}$$
$$\cdots \cdots \cdots \cdots \cdots \cdots \cdots$$
$$a_{m1}x_1 + a_{m2}x_2 + \cdots a_{mn}x_n = y_m$$

We can define the transpose of a matrix A as the matrix obtained by writing out the rows of A as columns. The transpose of A is denoted by A'. The (i, j) element of A' is the (j, i) element of A for all i, j. In particular, the transpose of a column vector is a row vector. Let x' denote the row vector $(x_1, \ldots x_m)$ and y' the row vector $(y_1, \ldots, y_m)$ then the set of equations can be written simply as a matrix equation $y = Ax$. We get the same relations from $y' = x'A'$.

The operations of matrix multiplication satisfy the following rules:

1. $A + B = B + A$
2. $A + (B + C) = (A + B) + C$
3. $\lambda(A + B) = \lambda A + \lambda B$, $(\lambda + \mu)A = \lambda A + \mu A$ where λ, μ are scalers
4. $A(BC) = (AB)C$
5. $A(B + C) = AB + AC$.

However, in general $AB \neq BA$. For example, if $A = \begin{bmatrix} 1 & 2 \\ 4 & 3 \end{bmatrix}$ and $B = \begin{bmatrix} 2 & 3 \\ 4 & 2 \end{bmatrix}$ then $AB = \begin{bmatrix} 10 & 7 \\ 20 & 18 \end{bmatrix}$ and $BA = \begin{bmatrix} 14 & 13 \\ 12 & 14 \end{bmatrix}$.

It is possible to define an identity matrix, I, such that $AI = IA = A$ for all conformable matrices. The identity matrix is a square matrix (of appropriate size) with 1's down the principal

$$I = \begin{bmatrix} 1 & & 0 \\ & \ddots & \\ 0 & & 1 \end{bmatrix}$$

diagonal and zeros elsewhere. This matrix is a special case of diagonal matrices which have any elements (from a given algebra) down the principal diagonal with zeros elsewhere. Having defined an identity matrix, the question naturally arises of whether all matrices have inverse matrices, that is, for a given matrix A, is there a matrix B such that $AB = BA = I$. In general matrices do not have inverses.

In order to discuss this further we need to consider the topic of determinants. For each square matrix there is a corresponding scalar quantity called the determinant of the matrix. Basically, this is the 'sum' of all the products of elements taking one from each row and column. The word sum was put in inverted commas, as some of these products are subtracted (or multiplied by -1 before being added). For example, consider a simple 2×2 matrix $A = \begin{bmatrix} a_{11} & a_{12} \\ a_{21} & a_{22} \end{bmatrix}$, then the determinant of

A, written $|A| = a_{11}a_{22} - a_{12}a_{21}$. For a 3×3

$$\text{matrix } A = \begin{bmatrix} a_{11} & a_{12} & a_{13} \\ a_{21} & a_{22} & a_{23} \\ a_{31} & a_{32} & a_{33} \end{bmatrix}$$

$$|A| = a_{11}\begin{vmatrix} a_{22} & a_{23} \\ a_{32} & a_{33} \end{vmatrix} - a_{12}\begin{vmatrix} a_{21} & a_{23} \\ a_{31} & a_{33} \end{vmatrix} + a_{13}\begin{vmatrix} a_{21} & a_{22} \\ a_{31} & a_{32} \end{vmatrix}$$

$$= (a_{11}a_{22}a_{33} - a_{11}a_{23}a_{32}) - (a_{12}a_{21}a_{33} - a_{12}a_{23}a_{31})$$
$$+ (a_{13}a_{21}a_{32} - a_{13}a_{22}a_{31}).$$

In calculating the determinant we started from the first row. For the element a_{11}, we removed the row and column containing a_{11} and constructed the determinant of the remaining 2×2 matrix. Similarly for the second element in that row, we removed the row and column containing it and found the determinant of the remaining matrix and subtracted it from what we have. We do the same for the remaining element in the row and add the result to our sum. We could have started by using any row or column, and the sign of each product is given by continuing the alternating $+$ and $-$ signs throughout the matrix.

Suppose then we start with the ith row of a general $m \times m$ matrix A. Then corresponding to the element a_{ij} there is a matrix obtained by removing the ith row and j^{th} column. We denote this matrix by A_{ij} and its determinant by $|A_{ij}|$. The determinant of A is then $\sum\limits_{i=1}^{n} (-1)^{i+j}a_{ij}|A_{ij}|$ and we would proceed to find $|A_{ij}|$ in the same way. The elements $|A_{ij}|$ are called *minors* and the elements $c_{ij} = (-1)^{i+j}|A_{ij}|$ are called *co-factors*. It is clear from the procedure for obtaining the determinant of an $m \times m$ matrix that no element can enter a particular product more than once and no two elements from the same row or column can do so either. If the expansion of $|A|$ for a 3×3 matrix A (above) is examined, we have 6 product terms and each involves elements from one row and one column.

We can now form for the matrix A the *adjoint of A*, which is another matrix whose elements are the co-factors of A, that is

$$\text{adj}(A) = \begin{bmatrix} c_{11} \cdots c_{1m} \\ \cdot \\ \cdot \\ \cdot \\ c_m \quad\quad c_{mm} \end{bmatrix} = [c_{ij}]$$

The inverse of A is given by: $A^{-1} = (1/|A|)\,\text{adj}(A)$.

If $|A| = 0$ this definition is meaningless and no inverse can be found. If a matrix A has its determinant $|A| = 0$ it is called a *singular matrix*, and if $|A| \neq 0$ it is a *non-singular matrix*. Every non-singular matrix defined over a field has an inverse and every singular matrix has no inverse. If a matrix A has an inverse, the inverse is easily shown to be unique and is denoted by A^{-1}.

A permutation matrix has only 0's and 1's as entries. Each row and each column contains only a single 1 and 0's elsewhere. For example, P_1 and P_2 are permutation matrices.

$$P_1 = \begin{bmatrix} 0 & 1 & 0 \\ 1 & 0 & 0 \\ 0 & 0 & 1 \end{bmatrix} \quad P_2 = \begin{bmatrix} 0 & 0 & 1 \\ 1 & 0 & 0 \\ 0 & 1 & 0 \end{bmatrix} \quad \text{and} \quad M = \begin{bmatrix} 2 & 1 & 2 \\ 3 & 2 & 4 \\ 0 & 1 & 2 \end{bmatrix}$$

Consider the four matrices P_1M, MP_1, P_2M and MP_2.

$$P_1M = \begin{bmatrix} 3 & 2 & 4 \\ 2 & 1 & 2 \\ 0 & 1 & 2 \end{bmatrix} \quad MP_1 = \begin{bmatrix} 1 & 2 & 2 \\ 2 & 3 & 4 \\ 1 & 0 & 2 \end{bmatrix}$$

$$P_2M = \begin{bmatrix} 0 & 1 & 2 \\ 2 & 1 & 2 \\ 3 & 2 & 4 \end{bmatrix} \quad MP_2 = \begin{bmatrix} 1 & 2 & 2 \\ 2 & 4 & 3 \\ 1 & 2 & 0 \end{bmatrix}$$

It is clear that both the matrices P_1M and P_2M are obtained by rearranging the rows of M. Similarly MP_1 and MP_2 are obtained by rearranging the columns of M. In general, premultiplying a matrix by a permutation rearranges the rows of a matrix, and postmultiplying by a permutation matrix rearranges the columns. It is clear that the identity matrix I is a permutation matrix (that leaves the rows and columns of a matrix where they are). Consider now the matrices P_1P_2 and $(P_1P_2)M$.

$$(P_1P_2) = \begin{bmatrix} 1 & 0 & 0 \\ 0 & 0 & 1 \\ 0 & 1 & 0 \end{bmatrix} \quad (P_1P_2)M = \begin{bmatrix} 2 & 1 & 2 \\ 0 & 1 & 2 \\ 3 & 2 & 4 \end{bmatrix}$$

It is clear that P_1P_2 is also a permutation matrix. In general, the set of permutation matrices of a given order ($n \times n$) form a group.

Suppose now we have a vector $V = [1, 2, 3]$. The product VP_1 exists and is the vector $[2, 3, 1]$ which is a simple rearrangement of V. If for the moment we forget the matrix, the second vector is a reordering of the first. The operation that does this rearrangement is called a permutation, and the matrix is a convenient representation for this. For a finite vector (n-tuple) there is only a finite number of permutations and these form an algebraic group.

Appendix D
Clique-Detection Algorithm

Step 1: Calculate the matrix C. (The graph C is either a partial graph of G, or a subgraph of a partial graph of G.)

Step 2: Examine the row sums of C.

If $\sum_{j=1}^{N} C_{ij} = n_i(n_i - 1)$ where n_i is an integer then the point i is unicliqual.

If there is such a point P, go to step 3.

If there is no such point, go to step 6.

Step 3: Let C_p be the clique in which P is unicliqual. (These are all the points with non-zero entries in C in the row corresponding to the point P.)

If $C_p = C$ (there is only one clique in the structure that the matrix C represents) go to step 9.

If $C_p \neq C$ go to step 4.

Step 4: Construct C_p' which is the set of unicliqual points (including p) in the clique C_p. Go to step 5.

Step 5: Let $C_1 = C - C_p'$ (C_1 is the subgraph of C obtained by removing the points of C_p'). Go to step 1.

Step 6: (There are no unicliqual points in C.) Select a (the) point with minimal row sum in C. Let this point be P. Go to step 7.

Step 7: Construct two groups $C(P)$ and $C(\bar{P})$ as follows:

(i) $C(P)$ is the subgroup of all points cocliqual with P.

(ii) $C(\bar{P})$ is the subgroup of all points in cliques that do not contain P.

(This is done by examining the entries of $C^2 \times C$.)

Note that

(i) $C(P) \cap C(\bar{P}) \neq \phi$.

(ii) There can be no clique simultaneously within $C(P)$ and $C(\bar{P})$, otherwise a clique can contain and not contain the same point. No clique can be split so that part is in $C(P)$ and part in $C(\bar{P})$. Go to step 8.

Step 8: Store groups constructed in step 7. Go to step 9.

Step 9: Take any group from storage and go to step 1. When the store is empty, stop.

The following (hypothetical) example is a simple one used to illustrate the algorithm.

$$\text{Let } G = \begin{array}{c} a \\ b \\ c \\ d \\ e \\ f \\ g \\ h \\ i \\ j \end{array}
\begin{bmatrix}
0 & 1 & 1 & 1 & 0 & 1 & 0 & 1 & 0 & 1 \\
1 & 0 & 0 & 1 & 1 & 1 & 1 & 0 & 0 & 1 \\
1 & 0 & 0 & 0 & 1 & 1 & 0 & 0 & 0 & 1 \\
1 & 1 & 0 & 0 & 0 & 1 & 0 & 0 & 0 & 0 \\
0 & 1 & 1 & 0 & 0 & 1 & 1 & 0 & 1 & 0 \\
1 & 1 & 1 & 1 & 1 & 0 & 0 & 0 & 0 & 1 \\
0 & 1 & 0 & 1 & 1 & 0 & 0 & 0 & 1 & 0 \\
1 & 0 & 0 & 0 & 0 & 0 & 0 & 0 & 0 & 0 \\
0 & 1 & 0 & 0 & 1 & 1 & 1 & 0 & 0 & 0 \\
1 & 1 & 1 & 1 & 0 & 1 & 0 & 0 & 0 & 0
\end{bmatrix}
\quad
\begin{array}{c}\text{then} \\ S = G \times G' =\end{array}
\begin{bmatrix}
0 & 1 & 1 & 1 & 0 & 1 & 0 & 1 & 0 & 1 \\
1 & 0 & 0 & 1 & 1 & 1 & 1 & 0 & 0 & 1 \\
1 & 0 & 0 & 0 & 1 & 1 & 0 & 0 & 0 & 1 \\
1 & 1 & 0 & 0 & 0 & 1 & 0 & 0 & 0 & 0 \\
0 & 1 & 1 & 0 & 0 & 1 & 1 & 0 & 1 & 0 \\
1 & 1 & 1 & 1 & 1 & 0 & 0 & 0 & 0 & 1 \\
0 & 1 & 0 & 0 & 1 & 0 & 0 & 0 & 1 & 0 \\
1 & 0 & 0 & 0 & 0 & 0 & 0 & 0 & 0 & 0 \\
0 & 0 & 0 & 0 & 1 & 0 & 1 & 0 & 0 & 0 \\
1 & 1 & 1 & 0 & 0 & 1 & 0 & 0 & 0 & 0
\end{bmatrix}$$

$$S^2 \times S = \begin{bmatrix}
0 & 3 & 2 & 2 & 0 & 4 & 0 & 0 & 0 & 3 \\
3 & 0 & 0 & 2 & 2 & 4 & 1 & 0 & 0 & 2 \\
2 & 0 & 0 & 0 & 1 & 3 & 0 & 0 & 0 & 2 \\
2 & 2 & 0 & 0 & 0 & 2 & 0 & 0 & 0 & 0 \\
0 & 2 & 1 & 0 & 0 & 2 & 2 & 0 & 1 & 0 \\
4 & 4 & 3 & 2 & 2 & 0 & 0 & 0 & 0 & 3 \\
0 & 1 & 0 & 0 & 2 & 0 & 0 & 0 & 1 & 0 \\
0 & 0 & 0 & 0 & 0 & 0 & 0 & 0 & 0 & 0 \\
0 & 0 & 0 & 0 & 1 & 0 & 1 & 0 & 0 & 0 \\
3 & 2 & 2 & 0 & 0 & 3 & 0 & 0 & 0 & 0
\end{bmatrix}$$

therefore

										row sum
$C =$										
a	0	3	2	2	0	4	0	0	3	14
b	3	0	0	2	2	4	1	0	2	14
c	2	0	0	0	1	3	0	0	2	8
d	2	2	0	0	0	2	0	0	0	6
e	0	2	1	0	0	2	2	1	0	8
f	4	4	3	2	2	0	0	0	3	18
g	0	1	0	0	2	0	0	1	0	4
i	0	0	0	0	1	0	1	0	0	2
j	3	2	2	0	0	3	0	0	0	10

The point h was the only one discarded in constructing the matrix C. In step 2 the element i is the only unicliqual element (its row sum is $n_i(n_i - 1) = 2$ for $n_i = 2$). The two points e and g correspond to non-zero entires in i's row and are therefore, cocliqual with i. The first clique detected is thus $\{e, g, i\}$. The element d has row sum $6 = 3.2$ and is therefore unicliqual in the clique $\{a, b, d, f\}$. The points i and d are the only unicliqual

$$G_1 = \begin{array}{c} a \\ b \\ c \\ e \\ f \\ g \\ j \end{array}
\begin{bmatrix}
1 & 1 & 1 & 0 & 1 & 0 & 1 \\
1 & 1 & 0 & 1 & 1 & 1 & 1 \\
1 & 0 & 1 & 1 & 1 & 0 & 1 \\
0 & 1 & 1 & 1 & 1 & 1 & 0 \\
1 & 1 & 1 & 1 & 0 & 0 & 1 \\
0 & 1 & 0 & 1 & 0 & 1 & 0 \\
1 & 1 & 1 & 0 & 1 & 0 & 0
\end{bmatrix}
\rightarrow S_1 =
\begin{bmatrix}
0 & 1 & 1 & 0 & 1 & 0 & 1 \\
1 & 0 & 0 & 1 & 1 & 1 & 1 \\
1 & 0 & 0 & 1 & 1 & 0 & 1 \\
0 & 1 & 1 & 0 & 1 & 1 & 0 \\
1 & 1 & 1 & 1 & 0 & 0 & 1 \\
0 & 1 & 0 & 1 & 0 & 0 & 0 \\
1 & 1 & 1 & 0 & 1 & 0 & 0
\end{bmatrix}$$

								row sum
$\rightarrow C_1 =$								
a	0	2	2	0	3	0	3	10
b	2	0	0	2	3	1	2	10
c	2	0	0	1	3	0	2	8
e	0	2	0	4	2	1	0	9
f	3	3	3	2	0	0	3	14
g	0	1	0	1	0	0	0	2
i	2	2	2	0	2	0	0	8

points in G, and we start again with $G_1 = \{a, b, c, e, f, g, j\}$. The element g is unicliqual in the clique $\{b, e, g\}$. No other element is unicliqual and we go back to step 1, with $G_2 = \{a, b, c, e, f, j\}$. The matrix C_2 is:

$$
\begin{array}{c}
 \\
a \\
b \\
c \\
e \\
f \\
j
\end{array}
\begin{bmatrix}
0 & 2 & 2 & 0 & 3 & 3 \\
2 & 0 & 0 & 1 & 3 & 2 \\
2 & 0 & 0 & 1 & 3 & 2 \\
0 & 1 & 1 & 0 & 2 & 3 \\
3 & 3 & 3 & 2 & 0 & 3 \\
3 & 2 & 2 & 0 & 3 & 0
\end{bmatrix}
\begin{array}{c}
\text{row} \\
\text{sum} \\
10 \\
8 \\
8 \\
7 \\
14 \\
10
\end{array}
$$

There are no unicliqual points in G_2 and we move to the construction of groups in step 7. The point e has minimal row sum and we form $C(e) = \{a, b, e, f\}$ and $C(\bar{e}) = \{a, b, c, f, j\}$. The algorithm is then straightforwardly performed on the two con-

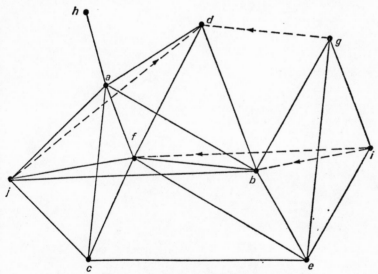

Figure D.1 Clique structure of G

structed groups to give the remaining cliques: $\{b, e, f\}$; $\{c, e, f\}$; $\{a, b, f, j\}$ and $\{a, c, f, j\}$. For this group G of 10 points there are no less than seven cliques, although no clique has more than four points in it. The graph for G is in Figure D.1 where the dashed lines are unreciprocated and not involved in any clique. With such an overlap of cliques it is possible (for small graphs) to examine where these small cliques would have coalesced into larger cliques but for the absence of lines. In our example $\{b, e, i, g\}$ would have formed a clique if the line (bi) were present. This shows how stringent are the demands of our definition of a clique. These four points are clearly clustered together but they would not form a clique. It is for configurations like this that the other definitions of cliques have been used.

Notes

1   *Introduction*

1   See, for example, Gouldner (1962) and Boalt (1969) for discussions of this issue. It is an issue that is far more complex than this and my position would be disputed by other sociologists and by some philosophers.

2   This is without having to decide whether or not the social order so achieved is coercive of individuals within that social order.

3   This is too brief. For a fuller and more adequate discussion see especially Parsons (1951), Smelser (1967, introduction), and also Olsen (1968).

4   The term prediction also covers cases of prediction of events that have already occurred on the basis of evidence prior to their occurrence.

2   *Relations*

1   All of the examples are empirical, but the last one is not affected by the subsequent discussion. The elements that each refers to are not always present. The people of Britain is not a fixed number of people as the demographic facts of birth, death and migration continually change the composition of this collection of people. Conceptually we know what precisely we are referring to, but empirically this is not strictly true. If we specify a particular instant of time, the composition will be fixed.

2   By specifying closely what is meant by each term, the difficulty of footnote 1 may be overcome. The definitions may be arbitrary (which is inconsequential) but they must be precise. This problem is not peculiar to our examples. For example $A = \{a | a$ is a number $< 10\}$ can at first sight pass for a set, but strictly speaking we have to specify what we mean by a number.

3   The set $\{i\}$ is simply an index set which is used to distinguish
      notationally one element of S from another.
4   If we were only interested in people over 21 then the first two
      elements do not form part of the variable. However, to avoid
      confusion, we shall use S as the variable rather than a subset of S.
5   If A and B were sets of numbers (corresponding to the given
      age ranges) then $A \cup B$ would be also a set of numbers. In our
      example the ages 16, 25, 21 and 30 are not included in the
      'over' and 'under' of A and B respectively.
6   If the v_i is an element of a set and not a set in its own right, we
      can write $V = \{\{v_i\}\}$ where $\{v_i\}$ denotes the set consisting of
      one element, namely v_i, we have a partition of V.
7   This discussion has ignored continuous variables. These vari-
      ables are taken up in Chapter 3 where measurement is considered.
8   The concept of ordering is not restricted to pairs. An ordered
      n-tuple $\langle a_1, a_2, \ldots a_n \rangle$ is n elements ordered in a particular way.
      Formally, an ordered pair is defined as $\langle a, b \rangle = \{\{a\}, \{a, b\}\}$.
      Although it appears intuitively obvious that $\langle a, b \rangle = \langle c, d \rangle$
      if and only if $a = c$ and $b = d$, this cannot be proved using the
      informal definition.
9   Again the provisos of footnotes 1 and 2 are necessary and will
      be assumed from now on. Notice that death does not affect this
      relation in terms of this particular property.
10   For a given set A and a given R the properties of the relation
      can always be determined unambiguously. The ambiguity arises
      from trying to talk of all friendship groups simultaneously.
      The properties of these sociometric relations are empirical and
      can only be decided for each specific set A (and R).
11   Clearly this relation is dependent upon our ability to talk of
      power in these terms. In number theory the equality of two
      numbers a and b is often proved by showing $a \supseteq b$ and $b \supseteq a$.
      For real numbers, these can only be satisfied simultaneously if
      $a = b$.
12   The mapping $m: A \to B$ is 1-1 if $m(a_1) = m(a_2)$ implies
      $a_1 = a_2$.

3   *Measurement*
1   References to sources dealing with particular techniques are
      given at the end of the chapter.

2   The ordering is not really necessary as long as we know that
     particular relations are defined for a given O and that we use
     the R_i consistently.
3   The number of sets involved in such a Cartesian product need
     not be restricted to two.
4   These mappings are, strictly, examples of a measurement
     operation and can therefore be regarded as part of the topic
     we are discussing.
5   Structural measurement can be regarded as a mapping
     $m: \hat{O} \to \hat{M}$, as the social relations are defined over the set of
     empirical objects.
6   By 'these' is meant any of the properties listed under reflexivity,
     symmetry and transitivity.
7   For example, if M is the set of real numbers, each of the
     nominal, ordinal interval and ratio scales are given by different
     sets of relations $T = \{T_i\}$.
8   If we consider the positive and negative real numbers then
     $f(x) = x^2$ preserves order, but only for positive numbers. If
     we include the negative numbers $f(-x) = x^2$ and order is not
     preserved. The transformation given by $f(x) = x^3$ preserves
     order for both positive and negative numbers.
9   Note that this is a statement about the properties of measure-
     ment structures and not the actual process of mapping.
10   The odd one out is population/dwelling units and it correlates
     negatively with the composite variable also.

4   Social Structure: Relations and Graphs

1   Kroeber's comment is taken from a quotation in Nadel (1957).
     Nadel lists and discusses various definitions of structure that
     have been employed by anthropologists. A similar profusion
     of definitions characterises sociology.
2   Nadel argues that it is preferable to limit the meaning of the
     term social structure rather than discard it altogether. The
     model suggested here is more abstract than those of Nadel or
     Frielich (1964). Nadel distinguishes between the general
     concept of role and specific behaviour of individuals in a con-
     crete social group. This is a necessary distinction. However
     both can be analysed in terms of graph theory and related
     ideas.

3   This use of a model is fully in accord with that of Nadel. There is no necessity for each $R_i \in R$ to be a relation onto S. In particular cases the properties of the social relations can be determined or sometimes postulated.

4   The conceptual framework at the beginning of this chapter should prove helpful in extending analyses of structure.

5   The question of the suitability of a group structure with respect to certain goals has been raised in a variety of contexts. For example, it has been raised as an issue in organisation theory pertaining to increase of efficiency and profits, and also by Lenin over the operation of a revolutionary party.

6   We need to determine whether there are leaders and what their structural location is (see for example, Starbuck, 1965).

7   Note that a relation and not a mapping is used (cf. footnote 3). Frequently one point has many lines directed out from it. Other points may have no lines incident from them.

8   See Forsyth and Katz (1946) and Luce and Perry (1949). It is interesting to note that Moreno, who initiated sociometry (see Moreno ed. 1960), was reluctant to accept matrix algebra as a source of techniques for analysing the sociogram, arguing that visual inspection was preferable. This view was rapidly shown to be untenable. It should be noted that many other representations of a graph can be made by use of matrices. For example, we could have the matrix representing incidence of lines with points which will, in general, be a rectangular matrix.

9   An alternative definition for a semipath is a set of points $s_1, s_2, \ldots s_k$ together with $k - 1$ lines, where only one line is taken from each pair $(s_1 s_2)$ or $(s_2 s_1)$, $(s_2 s_3)$ or $(s_3 s_2)$, $\ldots (s_{k-1} s_k)$ or $(s_k s_{k-1})$. The class of semipaths of a given graph will, by this definition, contain the paths of the graph. Those semipaths that are not paths are then called strict semipaths (see Harary, *et al.*, 1965).

10 In some books symmetrically complete graphs are described as complete. To avoid confusion the two concepts are distinguished here. For undirected graphs there can be no such distinction and we shall refer to complete graphs.

11 The representation of choices is a matter of convention. Subsequent studies have mainly used 0's and 1's and −1's to

represent indifference, positive choice and negative choice respectively. Entries on the main diagonal are usually taken as 0, thus ignoring self-choice and making the relation (and the graph) irreflexive.

12   This was the notion of a clique used by Forsyth and Katz and is employed also in the computerised routines.

13   Use of graph theory has been thought of as a means of by-passing the measurement problem (French, 1956). However, by attempting to have lines with differing values on them there arise questions as to how this can be achieved. In fact, use of graphs does not overcome the problem of measurement, as it rests upon a rather crude form of measurement; a dichotomised nominal (or ordinal) scale.

14   Alternatively a valued graph could be defined in terms of the set S and a relation from D to $S \times S$, where zero is a particular value in D which is assigned to pairs of points having no line between them.

15   Order is the only property of the integers of interest here. Any finite linearly ordered set with n elements can be put in a 1-1 correspondence with the first n integers. In this case $D = Z$, or a subset of Z.

16   A path at level n is a sequence of arcs such that the terminal point of one arc is the initial point in the succeeding arc, and the smallest valuation of any arc in the path is $\geqslant n$. We can go on to define 'connectedness at level n', and it is easily proved that the connectedness property at level n of V corresponds to the connectedness of V_n (see Doreian, 1969a for details).

17   The matrix $G = [g_{ij}]$ is not the group matrix as we have been using it, but its transpose is. Hubbell used the transpose of G in order to make his notation consistent with an input–output economic model he was generalising.

18   In fact stronger conditions are needed:

$$\sum_{j=1}^{N} |g_{ij}| \leqslant |(i = 1, 2, \ldots N)$$

with the strict inequality applying for at least one i in each strong component of the group structure.

19   A sequence of numbers $(a_1, a_2, \ldots a_n)$ tends to a limit λ as n tends to infinity, if given any positive number μ, however

small, we can find an integer N_μ such that all the terms of the sequence for $n_N = N_\mu$ lie between $\lambda - \mu$ and $\lambda + \mu$. If we have the series s_N where $s_N = \sum_{i=1}^{N} f_i$ then the partial sums s_N form a sequence. If this sequence tends to a limit then the series is convergent. [It can be noted that if a series is convergent it has a finite sum, and it does not follow that the sum of an infinite set of numbers is infinite. For example, the series $1 + \frac{1}{2} + \frac{1}{4} + \frac{1}{8} + \frac{1}{16} \ldots$ is a convergent series whose sum tends towards 2. It is through considering limits that one of Zeno's paradox (that if a tortoise is given a start in a race with Achilles, it can never be overtaken) is shown to be non-paradoxical.]

20   $\delta_{ij} = 1$ if $i = j$ and $\delta_{ij} = 0$ if $i = j$. In other words, the matrix $[\delta_{ij}]$ is simply the identity matrix I, as required.

21   The values of K are determined in terms of the group's total linkage strength.

22   The key theorem for the detection process is the following: If G is the group matrix and if the number of paths satisfying a 3-triple (α, β, γ) is s_{ij} for the points i and j, then $S = [s_{ij}] = G^\alpha \cdot d(G^\beta) \cdot G^\gamma$ (Berge, 1962, p. 134).

23   There are, however, many unresolved issues in their analysis (see, for example, Mechanic, 1968).

24   If there is a pair of points with no path between them in an undirected graph, the graph is disconnected. For a directed graph, if there is no path between two points in one direction this does not necessarily mean that the graph is disconnected. However, in this case, it is impossible to norm the various indices.

25   The majority of work done in this area stems from the work of Rapoport (see Rapoport, 1963). In deriving his distributions, especially values for connectivity he had to resort to approximations so that the mathematics remained tractable. Katz and Powell (1958) provide an approach without using approximations.

26   See Mitchell (1969) for an approach using graph theoretical tools to characterise networks in order to provide explanations for some social phenomena.

5   *Structural Balance*

1   There is considerable difficulty in deciding whether the struc-
     tures should all be objective, where each person is asked about
     the dyads that they are in, or subjective in that we consider the
     perceptions of individuals of the whole structure. If perception
     is accurate then the need for such a distinction vanishes.

2   Cartwright and Harary considered the case of an all negative
     3-cycle to be imbalanced.

3   The sign rule of multiplication is given in the simple table,

·	+1	−1
+1	+1	−1
−1	−1	+1

4   The same argument applies if we start in S_2 and the path
     contains a line from S_2 to S_1.

5   This is an arbitrary choice, but it makes no difference when the
     permanent is considered. In Chapter 4 the structure matrix was
     taken to have 0's in the main diagonal which is equivalent here
     to having the null relation in the main diagonal. Either p or o
     can be chosen without affecting the model. If a or n were chosen
     this would not be true. However, there is no rationale at all for
     using a or n in the main diagonal of the structure matrix. The
     choice on the main diagonal is arbitrary to the extent that it
     could be either p or o. In a belief structure it is reasonable to
     assume that a belief is positively related to itself.

6   They actually give six rules with the sixth stating: $A\ o\ B\ \&\ B\ r\ C$
     implies nothing about $A\ r\ C$. This has been clarified by Runkel
     and Peizer (1968) who define a universal relation that holds
     between all pairs. $A\ o\ B$ and $B\ r\ C$ implies $A\ j\ C$ where j is the
     universal relation.

7   This is a shortened form of 'pseudo-determinant'.

8   See Appendix C for the definition of a permutation. Each
     term of the product has one element from each row and
     column if R. Use of ψ precludes the possibility of having two
     elements from the same row or column in a single product
     term.

9   In the multiplication table there is a difference between O as
     the null relation and the O that appears in the table itself. The
     entry in the table is that for a line (r) followed by a null line.

There is no such path and the *o* refers to 'nothing'. The multiplication rules are not affected by this. See also Runkel and Peizer (1968).

10 Note that for both addition and multiplication, the inverse operations of subtraction and divisions are not uniquely defined.

11 For example, let R be the simple structure whose graph is G and whose matrix is R.

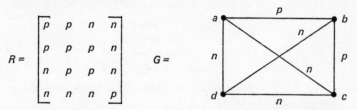

The product *nppn* corresponding to the 4-cycle (*dcbad*) appears in the permanent. So too does *ppnn* which corresponds to two 2-cycles (*aba*) and (*cdc*).

12 For a simple discussion of behaviour in triads, see Caplow (1968).

13 The first structure theorem can be restated for strongly connected graphs and can thus be made a little more general. (Fully complete graphs form a special case of strongly connected graphs.) Alternatively, we get the same result as a special case of the second structure theorem.

14 See Feather (1967) for a survey of experimental studies of balance in communication structures.

15 An easily proved theorem is one stating that a graph is balanced if and only if it is locally balanced at every point.

16 The indirect two-step paths $(+, -)$ and $(-, +)$ are not distinguished. The paths involving a null line $(0, 0)$, $(0, +)$ and $(0, -)$ are not included in the table as no prediction can be made about the direct line from them. 'Strengthened' (in Tables 5.3 and 5.4) denotes the fact that the direct and indirect paths are compatible whereas 'strained' means they are incompatible (according to the particular hypothesis in question).

17 See footnote 1. We can also examine whether perception within a dyad is balanced.

18   See Heider (1958), pp. 212–217.

19   Davis has values on arcs and defines the value of a cycle (or
      path) as the product of values on each arc in the cycle (or
      path). However, it is not clear what sociological meaning there
      is in such a product. By proceeding in two stages, Davis's
      results can be established by (i) using the signs and balance
      theory to predict change, and (ii) using the values in a secondary
      fashion in an attempt to predict where the changes will occur.
      Until we can introduce valuations properly into signed graphs,
      this is probably the best that can be done.

20   For example, Davis restricts his analysis to 'segmented' groups
      in the sense of Durkheim (1964). However, many of the
      hypotheses he derives were propounded in a context which, if
      anything, would be characterised as 'organic'. It may be that
      Durkheim's distinction is not particularly fruitful, but regard-
      less of this, the conditions for balance theory to be relevant
      have still not been specified closely by Davis.

21   See for example, the content of Cohn (1965).

6   *Formal Organizations*

1   Among the various suggestions are Cartwright (1959), and
     Oeser and Harary (1962, 1964). The article by Cartwright
     simply lists some graph theoretical terms and indicates how
     they might be useful. Harary discusses the notion of status
     where an individual's status is determined both by how many
     subordinates he has and how far they are below him. The two
     articles by Oeser and Harary present a mathematical model of
     role, which is more a model of task allocation, and as such, is
     of some value in discussing formal organisations.

2   One individual can occupy more than one position, and, one
     position can be responsible for more than one task. A position
     that is not responsible for any tasks may exist and such a
     sinecure can be formally represented.

3   The organisational chart is considered more fully in the fol-
     lowing section. However, it may be necessary to enquire
     whether or not the control exercised is legitimate. This in turn
     leads to a discussion of the role of rules and authority relations
     in an organisational structure. This is a separate (and im-

G

portant) discussion although it does not preclude the *analysis* of existing power structures.

4   The points where the structure is vulnerable are, in terms of graph theory, articulation points (or cut points). If they (or lines incident to them) are removed the graph becomes disconnected. In this context (organisations) they provide an example of liaison points discussed in Chapter 4.

5   See also Cartwright (1965) for a discussion of various influence structures that can be found within a formal organisation.

6   This section draws largely on the work of Friedell (1967).

7   Although some of the following material might be in part generalisable, there is an implicit restriction of the discussion to bureaucratic and commercial organisations.

8   Two levels that Cox considers separately are the specialist and trainee levels as they do not fit properly into the hierarchy of levels. One of the hypotheses listed by Udy (1965, p. 701) states that under conditions of (i) centralised planning and (ii) co-ordination being performed through the authority structure, the greater the technological complexity the more levels of administrative authority will there be in the organisation (with technological complexity held constant).

9   An alternative terminology is to call the two semilattices a join-semilattice and a meet-semilattice respectively.

10 The higher the level of technical knowledge required in an organisation, the more expertise will be considered as a basis for authority. (Udy, 1965, see also footnote 8.)

11 Strictly speaking this is a union-ideal that is defined for a union-semilattice. Another ideal can be defined for an intersection-semilattice (and both ideals can be defined for a lattice). However, we are only concerned here with union ideals.

7   Social Status

1   This too has been extensively studied and the variation between theories is characteristically large. Thus stratification can be seen as the result of shared core beliefs, or the values of society are seen as imposed by those who control society and have a monopoly of power.

2   See, for example, Warner and Lunt (1941): 'By class is meant

two or more orders of people who are believed to be, and are accordingly ranked by the members of the community, in socially superior and inferior positions' (p. 2).

3   There are numerous articles by Blalock that basically introduce into sociology the kind of problems that confront econometricians, and will confront sociologists more frequently in the future.

4   See also the remarks in Chapter 5 concerning this distinction. The legitimacy of such a status needs to be examined closely.

5   This section draws heavily upon the work of Fararo (1968, 1969, 1970). The reader is urged to study Fararo's work directly.

6   Strictly speaking if there was a C with this property then status in terms of invidious comparisons would not exist. If no status characteristic differentiates between individuals then we are dealing with a completely unstratified society.

7   The assumption that everybody uses the same states of C may be a dubious one. In this case the assumption could be dropped and the model made more complex in order to deal with this.

8   Note that E_a and π_a cannot change independently of each other. Once E_a has been defined, so too has π_a.

9   This clearly does not exhaust all of the possibilities.

10 Although the individuals involved are unlikely to use R (in Figure 7.1), it is possible to look at e rather than m in the following discussion. It may be the case that if a sociologist is studying the status chains that it is more convenient to make comparisons in the corresponding measurement structures.

11 For a full discussion see Cohn (1965).

12 The relevance of dimensions and their salience tends to be ignored by the rank theorists, who tend to assume that the dimensions they consider are relevant and salient.

8   *Social Mobility*

1   Piaggio's (1960) introduction to differential equations assumes knowledge of differential and integral calculus and co-ordinate geometry. Difference equations are easier to tackle and Goldberg (1957) provides an excellent introduction.

2   By using differential equations featuring transition coefficients,

Coleman provides a novel and perceptive analysis of contingency tables.

3   The existence of such convenient categories can be challenged as they may well be artefacts of a particular style of analysis. To the extent that they are artefacts, the utility of analyses based upon them is limited. The possibility of creating completely artificial mobility processes through our choice of categories highlights the danger of creating artefacts. In general, it is a problem that faces all social theorists.

4   A population is closed if no individuals leave the population and none enter it either.

5   This would simply mean that the mobility matrices are rectangular (and not square) matrices. For ease of presentation square matrices are used in this chapter. Difficulties that would arise for the use of rectangular matrices are indicated where necessary.

6   The notation becomes clearer when the mobility tables are written out (Figure 8.1).

7   Similar equations hold for the numbers of individuals in particular cells: $m_i = n_1 p_{1i} + n_2 p_{2i} + \cdots n_k p_{ki}, \ 1 \leqslant i \leqslant k$. (Note that $m_i = n_{\cdot i}$; the latter notation $(n_{\cdot i})$ is used for discussing the mobility matrix where it is more appropriate.)

8   For convenience, the categories are ordered from 1 (top) to k (bottom). Thus if $i < j$, the ith category is ordered above the jth category.

9   The matrix of proportions can be partitioned in the same way as the matrix of numerical values.

10 The areas she considered were: capital city, smaller cities, suburbs, industrial villages, mixed villages, agricultural villages and fishing villages.

11 The alternative notion of a completely immobile society is one where no one moves from his category. Here all the non-zero entries would be on the main diagonal.

12 This account is far too brief and incomplete. However as this goes beyond the scope of the book it is only mentioned here. The importance of this work must be stressed and can be found in Goodman (1965, 1969a, b)

13 The restriction to square matrices enters here. The states do not change during a Markov process. However, rectangular

transition matrices could be found for each time t, subject to the constraint that they are conformable for matrix multiplication. The assumption of a constant matrix for the use of Markov chains is clearly inapplicable for rectangular matrices.

14   If the transition matrix is regular (for some power r, P^r has no zero elements) then there exists a unique probability vector p which satisfies $p = pP$. If $p = (p_1, \ldots p_k)$ then $\lim_{n \to \infty} p_{ij} = p_i$ and P^∞ is of the form such that each column is the vector p'.

15   If B was not independent of grandfathers' occupation, the hypothesis $AB = C$ could still be satisfied.

9   *On the Prospects of Mathematical Sociology*

1   During the nineteenth century the use of mathematics in 'sociology' was one victim of a general reaction against positivism.

2   Criticism from hackneyed stereotypes of mathematics can justly be called trivial.

3   Note however, that it is not sufficient for a study of social relations.

4   If in the triad abc, $+3$ and -4 are the valuations on (ab) and (bc) respectively, what should the valuation of (ac) be in order for there to be balance? (Clearly the question is not restricted to these particular valuations.)

5   Davis's article is reprinted in this book.

6   These axioms were first included in an earlier edition of Kemeny *et al.* (1966).

7   Both patrilateral and matrilateral parallel cousin marriage is prohibited. For patrilateral parallel cousins to marry we need $M = W = C^{-1}C = I$, and similarly for matrilateral parallel cousins to marry we need $M = W = C^{-1}WW^{-1}C = I$. The notation of Figure 9.1 is standard. For a general introduction to kinship analysis the reader is referred to Fox (1967).

8   If $WC = CW$ and $CW = W^{-1}C$ then $WC = W^{-1}C$. Then $W = W^{-1}$ and $W^2 = I$.

9   For example if $W^2 = I$ and $W = C^3$ then there are six segments. See White (1963) for a complete classification. The axioms guarantee that $W^p = I$ and $C^m = I$ for finite p and m.

10   Anthropologists were highly critical of White's work (see, for example, Narroll, 1965). The criticism focusses on the lack of reality of the axioms and that kinship terminology is classified rather than kinship systems.

11   This M is not the marriage relation considered earlier.

12   Boyd thereby meets the major criticism made of White's work.

13   The second structure theorem (for connected graphs and therefore for strongly connected and complete graphs). By defining the composition of relations as a binary operation, $xABy$ if and only if there is a u such that xAu and uBy, Boyd also provides a means of generalising the work of Stinchcombe (1961).

14   In this section, I am not concerned with the philosophical debates over the hypothetico-deductive model of propositions and causality. Such issues are far from being irrelevant, but are extensively discussed elsewhere (see for example, Hempel, 1965 and Braithwaite, 1953).

15   The use of structural measurement is distinct to property measurement and it is the latter that is being considered here. Even so, structural measurement can also lead us to these questions especially when structure has to be related to other variables.

16   Equations of the form $Y = a + bx$ are linear equations with two variables.

17   For example we could have $D = b_1H^2 - b_1P^3$ which involves higher powers of particular variables. Alternatively we could consider $D = HP$ which is not a linear equation.

18   An introductory account is given by Abell (1970).

19   The work of Duncan (1966a) and Boyle (1970) are examples demonstrating how these problems are being tackled. Boyle's paper, together with an earlier paper (Boyle, 1966) is particularly important because it tackles the problem of using multivariate techniques to analyse data that do not satisfy the usual assumptions. We can also note that while Goodman (1969a, b) is primarily concerned with the analysis of mobility tables his techniques are much more generally applicable.

Bibliography

ABELL, P., 1968 (a) 'Measurement in Sociology: I. Measurement Systems', *Sociology*, Vol. 2, No. 1 (January) pp. 1–20.

ABELL, P., 1968 (b) 'Structural Balance in Dynamic Structures', *Sociology*, Vol. 2, No. 3 (September) pp. 333–52.

ABELL, P., 1969 'Measurement in Sociology: II. Measurement Structure and Sociological Theory', *Sociology*, Vol. 3, No. 3, pp. 397–411.

ABELL, P., 1970, *Introduction to Model Building in Sociology: Cross Sectional Models*, London, Weidenfeld and Nicolson (forthcoming).

ABELL, P. and DOREIAN, P., 1970, 'On the concept of Structure of Sociology' to be presented at the Annual Meeting of the British Assoc. for the advancement of Science, University of Durham.

ABELSON, R. P. and M. J. ROSENBERG, 1958 'Symbolic Psycho-logic: A Model of Attiduinal Cognition', *Behavioral Science*, Vol. 3, pp. 1–13.

ABELSON, R. P., et al., 1968 *Theories of Cognitive Consistency: A Source Book*, Chicago: Rand McNally.

ADAMS, E. W., 1966 'On the Nature and Purpose of Measurement', *Technical Report*, No. 4, April, 1966, University of Oregon.

ALKER, H. R. Jr, 1965 *Mathematics and Politics*, New York: MacMillan.

ANDERSON, T. W., 1954 'Probability Models for Analysing Time Changes in Attitudes', in *Mathematical Thinking in the Social Sciences*, P. F. Lazarsfeld (ed.), New York: Free Press in Glencoe.

ANDERSON, T. W. and L. A. GOODMAN, 1957 'Statistical Inference about Markov Chains', *Ann. Math. Stat.*, Vol. 28, pp. 89–110.

BALL, G. H., 1965 'Data Analysis in the Social Sciences: what about the details?', *AEIPS Conference Proceedings*, Vol. 27, Part I, 533–59.

BARNES, J. A., 1954 'Class and Committes in a Norwegian Island Parish', *Human Relations*, Vol. 7, pp. 39–58.

BARNES, J. A., 1969 'Graph Theory and Social Networks: a technical comment on connectedness and connectivity', *Sociology*, Vol. 3 (May), 1969, pp. 215–32.

BARTHOLOMEW, D. J., 1968 *Stochastic Models of Social Processes*, New York: Wiley.

BARTON, A. H. and B. ANDERSON, 1969 'Change in an Organisational System: Formalisation of a Qualitative Study', in Etzioni (ed.), 1969.

BARTOS, O., 1967 *Simple Models of Group Behaviour*, New York: Columbia University Press.

BAVELAS, A. A., 1948 'A Mathematical Model for Group Structures', *Applied Anthropology*, Vol. 7, pp. 16–30.

BAVELAS, A., 1950 'Communication in Task-Oriented Groups', *Journal of the Acoustical Society of America*, Vol. 22, pp. 725–30.

BEAUCHAMP, M. A., 1965 'An Improved Index of Centrality', *Behavioral Science*, Vol. 10, pp. 161–3.

BERELSON, B. R., *et al.*, 1954 *Voting: A Study of Opinion Formation in a Presidential Campaign*, Chicago: University of Chicago Press.

BERGE, C., 1962 *The Theory of Graphs and its Application*, New York: Wiley and Sons.

BERGER, J., *et al.*, 1962 *Types of Formalisation in Small-Group Research*, Boston: Houghton-Mifflin.

BERGER, J., M. ZELDITCH and B. ANDERSON, 1966 *Sociological Theories in Progress, Volume I*, Boston: Houghton-Mifflin.

BEUM, C. and E. C. BRUNDAGE, 1950 'A Method for Analysing the Sociomatrix', *Sociometry*, Vol. 13, pp. 141–5.

BILLEWICZ, W. Z., 1955 'Some Remarks on the Measurement of Social Mobility', *Population Studies*, Vol. 9, July, 1955, pp. 96–100.

BIRKELAND, E., 1967 'A Model for Predicting Educational Enrolment and Output in the Post-Secondary Educational System of Norway', The Norwegian Research Council for Science and the Humanities Research Department.

BIRKHOFF, G., 1966 *Lattice Theory* (3rd. ed.) Providence: American Mathematical Society.

BLALOCK, H. M. Jr, 1960 *Social Statistics*, New York: McGraw-Hill.

BLALOCK, H. M. Jr, 1964 *Causal Inference in Non-Experimental Research*, Chapel Hill: University of North Carolina Press.

BLALOCK, H. M. Jr, 1966 'The Identification Problem and Theory Building: The Case of Status Inconsistency', *American Sociological Review*, Vol. 31, (February), pp. 52–61.

BLALOCK, H. M. Jr, 1967 (a) 'Status Inconsistency and Interaction: Some Alternative Models', *American Journal of Sociology*, Vol. 73, No. 3, pp. 305–15.

BLALOCK, H. M. Jr, 1967 (b) 'Status Inconsistency, Social Mobility, Status Integration and Structural Effects', *American Sociological Review*, Vol. 32, pp. 790–801.

BLALOCK, H. M., 1969 (a) *Theory Construction*, Englewood Cliffs: Prentice Hall.

BLALOCK, H. M. Jr, 1969 (b) 'Multiple Indicators and the Causal Approach to Measurement Error', *American Journal of Sociology*, Vol. 75, No. 2, pp. 264–73.

BLALOCK, H. M. Jr, and A. BLALOCK (eds.), 1968 *Methodology in Social Research*, New York: McGraw-Hill.

BLAU, P. M. and DUNCAN, O. D., 1967 *The American Occupational Structure*, New York: Wiley.

BLUMEN, I., M. KOGAN and P. J. MCCARTHY, 1955 *The Industrial Mobility of Labor as a Probability Process*, Ithaca, New York: Cornell University Press.

BOALT, G., 1969 *The Sociology of Research*, Carbondale: Southern Illinois University Press.

BOTT, E., 1956 *Family and Social Network*, London: Tavistock.

BOYD, J. P., 1969 'The Algebra of Group Kinship', *Journal Math. Psy.* Vol. 6, No. 1 (February), pp. 139–67.

BOYLE, R. P., 1966 'Causal Theory and Statistical Measures of Effect: A Convergence', *American Sociological Review*, Vol. 31, pp. 834–51.

BOYLE, R. P., 1970 'Path Analysis and Ordinal Data', *American Journal of Sociology*, Vol. 75, No. 4 (January), pp. 461–95.

BRAITHWAITE, R. B., 1953 *Scientific Explanation*, Cambridge: Cambridge University Press.

BURNS, T. and G. M. STALKER, 1961 *The Management of Innovation*, London: Tavistock Publications.

CAPLOW, T., 1968 *Two Against One: Coalitions in a Triad*, Englewood Cliffs, New Jersey: Prentice-Hall.

CARLSSON, G., 1958 *Social Mobility and Class Structure*, Lund: Gleerup.

CARTWRIGHT, DORWIN and HARARY, F., 1956 'Structural Balance:

A Generalisation of Heider's Theory', *Psychological Review*, Vol. 63, No. 5, pp. 277–94.

CARTWRIGHT, DORWIN, 1959 'The Potential Contribution of Graph Theory to Organisation Theory', in Haire (ed.) 1959.

CARTWRIGHT, DORWIN, 1965 'Influence, Leadership, Control', in March (ed.) 1965, pp. 1–47.

CARTWRIGHT, D. and GLEASON, T., 1967 'The Number of Paths and Cycles in a Digraph', *Psychometrika*, 31, pp. 179–99.

CHOMSKY, N., 1963 'Formal Properties of Grammars', in Luce *et al.* (ed.) 1963, pp. 323–418.

CHOMSKY, N. and G. MILLER, 1963 'Finitary Models of Language Users' in Luce *et al.* (ed.) 1963, pp. 419–92.

COHN, P. M., 1965 *Universal Algebra*, New York: Harper.

COLEMAN, J. S., 1957 *Community Conflict*, New York: The Free Press of Glencoe.

COLEMAN, J. S., 1958 'Relational Analysis: The Study of Social Organisations with Survey Methods', *Human Organisation*, Vol. 17, pp. 28–36.

COLEMAN, J. S., 1964 *Introduction to Mathematical Sociology*, Glencoe: The Free Press of Glencoe.

COLEMAN, 1966 'Reward Structures and the Allocation of Effort' in Lazarsfeld and Henry (eds.) 1966, pp. 159–74.

COLEMAN, J. S., 1968 'The Mathematical Study of Change', in Blalock and Blalock (eds.) 1968.

COLEMAN, J. S., ELIHU KATZ and HERBERT MENZEL, 1966 *Medical Innovation*, Indianapolis: Bobbs-Merrill.

COLEMAN, J. S. and DUNCAN MACRAE Jr, 1960 'Electronic Processing of Sociometric Data for Group up to 1,000 in Size', *American Sociological Review*, Vol. 25 (October), pp. 722–7.

COOMBS, C. H., 1964 *A Theory of Data*, New York: Wiley.

COSTNER, H., 1969 'Theory, Deduction and Rules of Correspondence', *American Journal of Sociology*, Vol. 75, No. 2, pp. 245–63.

COSTNER, H. L. and R. K. LEIK, 1964 'Deductions from "axiomatic theory" ', *American Sociological Review*, Vol. 29 (December), pp. 819–35.

COX, JOAN, 1968 'Towards a Manpower Grid', paper read at the Manpower Planning Conference of the Industrial Society, 26 November 1968.

CUZZORT, R. P., 1969 *Humanity and Modern Sociological Thought*, New York: Holt, Rinehart and Winston.

DAVIS, J. A., 1963 'Structural Balance, Mechanical Solidarity and Interpersonal Relations', *American Journal of Sociology*, LXVIII, pp. 444–62. (Reprinted in Berger *et al.*, 1966.)

DAVIS, J. A., 1967 'Clustering and Structural Balance in Graphs', *Human Relations*, Vol. 20, pp. 181–8.

DOREIAN, PATRICK, 1969 (a) 'A Note on the Detection of Cliques in Valued Graphs', *Sociometry*, Vol. 32, No. 2 (June), pp. 237–42.

DOREIAN, PATRICK, 1969 (b) 'Interaction Under Conditions of Crisis: Applications of Graph Theory to International Relations', Peace Research Society Papers XI: The Budapest Conference, 1968, pp. 89–107.

DOREIAN, P., 1970 'Matrix Operations for valued graphs' (mimeo), University of Essex.

DOREIAN, P. and STOCKMAN, N., 1969 'A critique of the multi-dimensional approach to stratification', *Sociological Review*, Vol. 17 (March), pp. 47–65.

DUBIN, R., 1969 *Theory Building*, New York: The Free Press of Glencoe.

DUNCAN, O. D., 1961 'A Socioeconomic Index for all Occupations', in A. J. Reiss Jr, *et al. Occupations and Social Status*, New York: Free Press of Glencoe.

DUNCAN, O. D., 1966 (a) 'Path Analysis: Sociological Examples', *American Journal of Sociology*, Vol. 72, No. 1 (July), pp. 1–16.

DUNCAN, O. D., 1966 (b) 'Methodological Issues in the Analysis of Social Mobility', in N. J. Smelser and S. M. Lipset (eds.) 1966.

DURBIN, J., 1955 'Appendix Note on a Statistical Question Raised in the Preceding Paper', *Population Studies*, Vol. 9, July 1955, p. 101.

DURKHEIM, E., 1951 *Suicide* (Trans. J. A. Spalding and G. Simpson), New York: The Free Press of Glencoe.

DURKHEIM, E., 1964 *The Division of Labour in Society* (Trans. G. Simpson), New York: The Free Press of Glencoe.

ETZIONI, A., 1961 (a) *A Comparative Analysis of Complex Organisations*, New York: The Free Press of Glencoe.

ETZIONI, A. (ed.), 1961 (b) *Complex Organisations: A Sociological Reader*, New York: Holt, Rinehart and Winston Inc. (2nd ed. *A Sociological Reader on Complex Organisations*, 1969).

FARARO, T. J. and M. H. SUNSHINE, 1964 'A Study of a Biased Friendship Net', Youth Development Centre, Syracuse University.

FARARO, T. J., 1968 'Theory of Status', *General Systems*, Vol. XIII, pp. 177–188.

FARARO, T. J., 1969 'Status, Expectations and Situation: A Formulation of the Structure Theory of Status Characteristics and Expectation States' (mimeo), University of Pittsburgh.

FARARO, T. J., 1970 'Strictly stratified Systems', *Sociology*, Vol. 4, No. 1, pp. 85–104.

FEATHER, N. T., 1967 'A Structural Balance Approach to the Analysis of Communication Effects', in *Advances in Experimental Social Psychology*, Vol. 3, New York: Academic Press.

FELLER, W., 1957 *An Introduction to Probability Theory and Its Applications*, (2nd. ed.) New York: Wiley.

FESTINGER, L., 1949 'The Analysis of Sociograms Using Matrix Algebra', *Human Relations*, Vol. 2, pp. 153–8.

FESTINGER, L., 1954 'A Theory of Social Comparison Processes', *Human Relations*, Vol. 7, pp. 117–40.

FESTINGER, L., 1957 *Theory of Cognitive Dissonance*, Evanston: Row Peterson.

FLAMENT, C., 1963 *Applications of Graph Theory to Group Structure*, Englewood Cliffs, New Jersey: Prentice-Hall.

FORD, L. R. Jr and D. R. FULKERSON, 1962 *Flows in Networks*, Princeton, New Jersey: Princeton University Press.

FORSYTH, E. and KATZ, L., 1946 'A Matrix Approach to the Analysis of Sociometric Data', *Sociometry*, Vol. 9, pp. 340–7.

FOX, R., 1967 *Kinship and Marriage*, Harmondsworth: Penguin.

FRENCH, J. R. P. Jr, 1956 'A Formal Theory of Power', *Psych. Review*, Vol. 63, pp. 181–94.

FRIEDELL, M. F., 1967 'Organisations as Semilattices', *American Sociological Review*, Vol. 32 (February), pp. 46–54.

FRIELICH, M., 1964 'Towards a Model of Social Structure', *J. Roy. Anthrop. Inst.*, Vol. 94, pp. 183–200.

GALTUNG, J., 1964 'A Structural Theory of Aggression', *Journal of Peace Research*, Vol. 1, No. 1, pp. 36–54.

GALTUNG, J., 1966 'International Relations and International Conflicts: A Sociological Approach', *Transactions of the Sixth World Congress of Sociology*.

GALTUNG, J., 1967 *Theory and Methods of Social Research*, Oslo: Scandinavian University Books.

GLASS, D. V., 1954 *Social Mobility in Britain*, London: Routledge and Kegan Paul.

GOLDBERG, S., 1957 *Introduction to Differences Equations*, New York: Wiley.

GOODMAN, L. A., 1961 'Statistical Methods for the Mover-Stayer Model', *J. Am. Stat. Association*, Vol. 56, pp. 841–68.

GOODMAN, L. A., 1962 'Statistical Methods for Analysing Processes of Change', *American Journal of Sociology*, Vol. 68, pp. 57–78.

GOODMAN, L. A., 1965 'On the Statistical Analysis of Mobility Tables', *American Journal of Sociology*, Vol. LXX, No. 5, March, pp. 564–86.

GOODMAN, L. A., 1969 (a) 'How to ransack social mobility tables and other kinds of cross-classification tables', *American Journal of Sociology*, Vol. 75, No. 1, pp. 1–40.

GOODMAN, L. A., 1969 (b) 'On the Measurement of Social Mobility: An Index of Status Persistance', *American Sociological Review*, Vol. 55 (December), pp. 831–50.

GOODMAN, L. A. and W. H. KRUSKAL, 1954 'Measures of Association for Cross Classification', *J. Am. Stat. Association*, Vol. 49, pp. 723–64.

GOODMAN, L. A. and W. H. KRUSKAL, 1959 'II Further Discussion and References', *J. Am. Stat. Association*, Vol. 54, pp. 123–63.

GOODMAN, L. A. and W. H. KRUSKAL, 1963 'III Approximate Sampling Theory', *J. Amer. Stat. Association*, Vol. 58, pp. 310–64.

GOODSTEIN, R. L., 1963 *Boolean Algebra*, Oxford: Pergamon.

GOULDNER, A. W., 1954 *Patterns of Industrial Bureaucracy*, Antioch: Antioch Press.

GOULDNER, A. W., 1962 'Anti-Minotaur: The Myth of a Value-Free Sociology', *Social Problems*, Vol. 9, No. 3, pp. 199–213.

GREEN, B. F. Jr, 1954 'Attitude Measurement' in Lindzey, G. (ed.) *Handbook of Social Psychology*, *I. Theory and Method*, Reading, Mass.: Addison-Wesley.

GROSS, E., 1964 'On Controlling Marginals in Social Mobility Measurement', *American Sociological Review*, Vol. 29, pp. 886–7.

GROSSMAN, I. and W. MAGNUS, 1964 *Groups and their Graphs*, New York: Random House.

GUTTMAN, L., 1949 'The Basis for Scalogram Analysis' in Stouffer, S. *et al.*, *Measurement and Prediction*, Princeton: Princeton University Press.

HAGE, J., 1965 'An Axiomatic Theory of Organisations', *A.S.Q.*, Vol. 10 (December), pp. 289–320.

HAIRE, M. (ed.), 1959 *Modern Organisation Theory*, New York: Wiley.

HARARY, F. and I. C. ROSS, 1957 'A Procedure for Clique Detection Using the Group Matrix', *Sociometry*, Vol. 20, No. 3, September, pp. 205–16.

HARARY, F., 1959 (a) 'On the Measurement of Structural Balance', *Behavioral Science*, Vol. 4, No. 4, October, pp. 316–24.

HARARY, F., 1959 (b) 'Status and Contrastatus', *Sociometry*, Vol. 22, pp. 23–43.

HARARY, F., 1960 'A Matrix Criterion for Structural Balance', *Naval Research Logistics Quarterly*, Vol. 7, (No. 2), pp. 195–9.

HARARY, F., 1961 'A Structural Analysis of the Situation in the Middle-East', *Journal of Conflict Resolutions*, Vol. 5, pp. 167–78.

HARARY, F., R. Z. NORMAN and D. CARTWRIGHT, 1965 *Structural Models: An Introduction to the Theory of Directed Graphs*, New York: Wiley.

HEIDER, F., 1946 'Attitudes and Cognitive Organisation', *Journal of Psychology*, Vol. 21, pp. 107–12.

HEIDER, F., 1957 *The Psychology of Interpersonal Relations*, New York: Wiley.

HEMPEL, C. G., 1952 'Fundamentals of Concept Formation in Empirical Science', in *International Encyclopedia of Unified Science*, Chicago: University of Chicago Press.

HEMPEL, C. G., 1965 *Aspects of Scientific Exploration and Other Essays in the Philosophy of Science*, New York: The Free Press of Glencoe.

HOMANS, G. C., 1950 *The Human Group*, New York: Harcourt, Brace and Co.

HODGE, R. W., 1966 'Occupational Mobility as a Probability Process', *Demography*, Vol. 3, No. 1, pp. 19–34.

HØIVIK, T. and NILS PETTER GLEDITSCH, 1968 'Structural Parameters of Graphs' (mimeo), Publication M.5. International Peace Research Institute, Oslo.

HOPKINS, T. M., 1964 *The Exercise of Influence in Social Groups*, Totowa N.T.: Bedminster Press.

HUBBELL, C. H., 1965 'An input–output approach to clique identification', *Sociometry*, Vol. 28, pp. 377–99.

JACKSON, E. F. and R. F. CURTIS, 1968 'Conceptualisation and Measurement in the Study of Social Stratification', in Blalock and Blalock (ed.) 1968, pp. 112–49.

JOHNSTON, J., 1963 *Econometric Methods*, New York: McGraw Hill.

KATZ, L. and J. H. POWELL, 1955 'Measurement of the Tendency towards Reciprocation of Choice', *Sociometry*, Vol. 18, pp. 659–65.

KEMENY, J. G. and J. L. SNELL, 1962 *Mathematical Models in the Social Sciences*, Boston: Ginn and Co.

KEMENY, J. G., J. L. SNELL and G. L. THOMPSON, 1966 *Introduction to Finite Mathematics* (2nd. ed.), Englewood Cliffs, New Jersey: Prentice-Hall.

KENDALL, M. G., 1955 *Rank Correlation Methods* (2nd. ed.), London: Griffin.

KERLINGER, F. N., 1964 *Foundations of Behavioural Research*, New York: Holt, Rinehart and Winston.

KEYFITZ, N., 1968 *Introduction to the Mathematics of Population*, Reading, Mass.: Addison-Wesley.

KLINE, M., 1953 *Mathematics in Western Culture*, London Oxford University Press.

KLINE, M. (ed.), 1969 *Mathematics in the Modern World* (readings from *Scientific American*), San Francisco: W. H. Freeman and Co.

KRUSKAL, W. H., 1958 'Ordinal Measures of Association', *J. Am. Stat. Association*, Vol. 58, pp. 814–61.

KRUSKAL, J. B., 1964 (a) 'Multidimensional Scaling by Optimising Goodness to Fit to a Nonmetric Hypothesis', *Psychometrika*, Vol. 29, No. 1 (March), pp. 1–27.

KRUSKAL, J. B., 1964 (b) 'Nonmetric Multidimensional Scaling: A Numerical Method', *Psychometrika*, Vol. 29, No. 2 (June), pp. 115–29.

LANDECKER, W., 1960 'Class Boundaries', *American Sociological Review*, Vol. 25, pp. 868–77.

LAZARSFELD, P. F., 1954 'A Conceptual Introduction to Latent Structure Analysis', in Lazarsfeld, P. F. (ed.) *Mathematical Thinking in the Social Sciences*, New York: The Free Press of Glencoe.

LAZARSFELD, P. F., 1959 'Problems in Methodology', in Merton, R. K., Broom, L., and Cottrell, L. S. (eds.), *Sociology Today*, New York: Basic Books.

LAZARSFELD, P. F. and A. H. BARTON, 1951 'Qualitative Measurement in the Social Sciences', in Lerner, D. and H. D. Lasswell (eds.) *The Policy Sciences*, Stanford: Stanford University Press.

LAZARSFELD, P. F. and N. HENRY (eds.), 1966 *Readings in Mathematical Social Science*, Chicago: Science Research Associates.

LENSKI, G. E., 1954 'Status Crystallisation: A Non-Vertical Dimension of Status', *American Sociological Review*, Vol. 19, August, pp. 405–13.

LIPSCHUTZ, S., 1964 *Theory and Problems of Set Theory and Related Topics*, Schaum Publication Company, New York.

LIPSET, S. M., M. A. TROW and J. S. COLEMAN, 1956 *Union Democracy: The Internal Politics of the International Typographical Union*, New York: The Free Press of Glencoe.

LITTERER, J. A. (ed.), 1963 *Organisations: Structure and Behavior*, New York: Wiley.

LORD, F. M. and M. R. NOVIC, 1968 *Statistical Theories of Mental Test Scores*, Reading, Mass.: Addison-Wesley.

LOUNDSBURY, F. G., 1964 'A Formal Account of the Crow and Omaha-Type Kinship Terminologies', in Goodenough, L. W. (ed.) *Explorations in Cultural Anthropology: Essays in honor of George Peter Murdock*, New York: McGraw-Hill, pp. 351–93.

LUCE, R. D. and A. D. PERRY, 1949 'A Method of Matrix Analysis of Group Structure', *Psychometrika*, Vol. 14, pp. 95–116.

LUCE, R. D. and H. RAIFFA, 1957 *Games and Decisions*, New York: Wiley.

LUCE, R. D. *et al.* (ed.), 1963 *Handbook of Mathematical Psychology*, Vol. 2, New York: Wiley.

LUCE, R. D. and J. W. TUCEY, 1964 'Simultaneous Conjoint Measurement: A New Type of Fundamental Measurement', *Journal of Mathematical Psychology*, Vol. 1, pp. 248–77.

LUCE, R. D., 1966 'Two Extensions of Conjoint Measurement', *Journal of Mathematical Psychology*, Vol. 3, pp. 348–70.

LUCHINS, A. S. and E. H. LUTCHINS, 1965 *Logical Foundations of Mathematics for Behavioral Scientists*, New York: Holt, Rinehart and Winston.

MARCH, J. G. and H. A. SIMON, 1958 *Organisations*, New York: Wiley.

MARCH, J. G. (ed.), 1965 *Handbook of Organisations*, Chicago: Rand McNally.

MATRAS, JUDAH, 1960 'Comparisons of Intergenerational Occupational Mobility Patterns: An Application of the Formal Theory of Social Mobility', *Population Studies*, Vol. XIV, No. 2, November, pp. 163–9.

MATRAS, JUDAH, 1961 'Differential Fertility, Intergenerational Occupational Mobility and Change in Occupational Distributions: Some Elementary Interrelationships', *Population Studies*, Vol. XV, No. 2, November, pp. 187–97.

MATRAS, JUDAH, 1967 'Social Mobility and Social Structure: Some Insights from the Linear Model', *American Sociological Review*, Vol. 32, August, pp. 608–14.

McCLEERY, R. H., 1957 *Policy Change in Prison Management*, East Lansing: Michigan State University, Governmental Research Bureau.

McGINNIS, R., 1965 *Mathematical Foundations for Social Analysis*, Indianapolis: Bobbs-Merrill.

McGINNIS, R., 1968 'A Stochastic Model of Social Mobility', *American Sociological Review*, Vol. 33, pp. 712–22.

MECHANIC, D., 1967 'Review of Coleman *et al.* (1966)', *American Sociological Review*, Vol. 32, pp. 644–6.

MERTON, R. K., 1956 *Social Theory and Social Structure*, (rev. ed.), New York: The Free Press of Glencoe.

MINISTRY OF TECHNOLOGY, 1968 'The Element of Management in Job Classification' (mimeo), paper ES2 (68) 12.

MITCHELL, J. C. (ed.), 1969 *Social Networks in Urban Situations*, Manchester: Manchester University Press.

MORENO, J. L. (ed.), 1960 *The Sociometry Reader*, New York: The Free Press of Glencoe.

MOSTELLER, F., R. E. F. ROARKE and G. B. THOMAS Jr, 1961 *Probability and Statistics*, Reading, Mass.: Addison-Wesley.

NADEL, S. F., 1957 *The Theory of Social Structure*, London: Cohen and West.

NARROLL, R., 1965 'Review of White (1963)', *American Journal of Sociology*, Vol. 71, No. 2, pp. 217–18.

NEWCOMBE, T. M., 1953 'An Approach to Communicative Acts', *Psychological Review*, Vol. 60, pp. 393–404.

OESER, O. A. and F. HARARY, 1962 'A Mathematical Model for Structural Role Theory I', *Human Relations*, Vol. 15, pp. 89–109.

OESER, O. A. and F. HARARY, 1964 'A mathematical Model for Structural Role Theory II', *Human Relations*, Vol. 17, pp. 3–22.

OLSEN, M. E., 1968 *The Process of Social Organisation*, New York: Holt, Rinehart and Winston.

ORE, O., 1962 *Theory of Graphs*, Providence: American Mathematical Society.

OSGOOD, C. E. and P. H. TANNENBAUM, 1955 'The Principle of Congruity in the Prediction of Attitude Change', *Psychological Review*, Vol. 62, pp. 42–55.

OSSOWSKI, S., 1963 *Class Structure in the Social Consciousness*, London: Routledge and Kegan Paul.

PARSONS, T., 1951 *The Social System*, New York: The Free Press of Glencoe.

PIAGGIO, H. T. H., 1960 *An Elementary Treatise on Differential Equations and Their Applications*, (revised edition), London: G. Bell and Sons.

PRAIS, S. J., 1955 'Measuring Social Mobility', *Journal of the Royal Statistical Society*, Series A., Vol. 118, pp. 56–66.

RAPOPORT, A., 1951 'Nets with Distance Bias', *Bull. Math. Biophysics*, Vol. 13, pp. 85–91.

RAPOPORT, A., 1963 'Mathematical Models of Social Interaction', in Luce, *et al.*, (ed.) 1963.

RAMSØY, NATALIE ROGOFF, 1966 'Changes in Rates and Forms of Mobility', in Smelser and Lipset (eds.), 1960.

REISSMAN, L., 1967 *Social Stratification*, in Smelser (ed.), 1967.

ROGERS, ANDRE, 1967 'A Markovian Policy Model of Interregional Migration' *Papers of the Regional Science Association*, Vol. 17, pp. 205–24.

ROGERS, A., 1968 *Matrix Analysis of Interregional Population Growth and Distribution*, Berkeley: University of California Press.

ROSS, I. C. and F. HARARY, 1952 'On the Determination of Redundancies in Sociometric Chains', *Psychometrika*, Vol. 17, No. 2, pp. 195–208.

ROSS, I. C. and F. HARARY, 1955 'Identification of the Liaison Persons of an Organisation Using the Structure Matrix', *Management Science*, Vol. 1, pp. 251–8.

ROSS, I. C. and F. HARARY, 1959 'A Description of Strengthening and Weakening Members of a Group', *Sociometry*, Vol. 22, No. 2, pp. 139–47.

RUNKEL, P. J and D B. PEIZER, 1968 'The Two Valued Orientation of Current Equilibrium Theory', *Behavioral Science*, Vol. 13, pp. 56–65.

SABIDUSSI, GERT, 1966 'The Centrality Index of a Graph', *Psychometrika*, Vol. 31, No. 4, pp. 581–603.

SCOTT, W., 1955 'Some Remarks on the Measurement of Social Mobility – A Reply', *Population Studies*, Vol. 9 (July), pp. 102–3.

SHAW, M. E., 1964 'Communication Networks', in *Advances in Experimental Social Psychology, Vol. I*, (Berkowitz, L., ed.), pp. 111–47.

SHEPARD, R. N., 1966 'Metric Structures in Ordinal Data' *J. Math. Psy.* Vol. 3, 287-315.

SIEGEL, S., 1956 *Non-parametric Methods for the Behavioral Sciences*, New York: McGraw-Hill.

SIMMEL, G., 1950 *The Sociology of George Simmel*, K. H. Wolff, Trans. (ed.), New York: The Free Press of Glencoe.

SIMON, H. A., 1957 *Models of Man*, New York: Wiley.

SMELSER, N. J. and S. M. LIPSET (eds.), 1966 *Social Structure and Social Mobility in Economic Development*, Chicago: Aldine.

SMELSER, N. J. (ed.), 1967 *Sociology: An Introduction*, New York: Wiley.

SOKAL, R. R. and P. H. A. SNEATH, 1963 *Principles of Numerical Taxonomy*, San Francisco: W. H. Freeman and Co.

SOROKIN, P. A., 1956 *Fads and Foibles in Modern Sociology*, Chicago: Henry Regnery and Co.

SPILERMAN, SEYMOUR, 1966 'Structural Analysis and the Generation of Sociograms', *Behavioral Science*, Vol. 11 (July), pp. 312–18.

STEVENS, S. S., 1951 'Mathematics, Measurement and Psychophysics', in Stevens, S. S., *Handbook of Experimental Psychology*, New York: Wiley.

STARBUCK, W. H., 1965 'Mathematics and Organisation Theory', in March (ed.), 1965, pp. 335–86.

STINCHCOMBE, A. L., 1961 'On the Use of Matrix Algebra in the Analysis of Formal Organisation', in Etzioni (ed.) 1961, 1st edition, pp. 478–84.

STINCHCOMBE, A. L., 1967 'Formal Organisations', in Smelser (ed.) 1967, pp. 151–202.

STINCHCOMBE, A. L. and T. R. HARRIS, 1969 'Independence and Inequality: A Specification of the Davis–Moore Theory', *Sociometry*, Vol. 22, No. 1, (March.)

SVALASTOGA, 1959 *Prestige, Class and Mobility*, London Heinemann.

TAYLOR, HOWARD F., 1967 'Balance and Change in the Two-Person Group', *Sociometry*, Vol. 30, No. 3, pp. 262–79.

TORGERSON, W. S., 1958 *Theory and Methods of Scaling*, New York: Wiley.

UDY, S. H. Jr, 1965 'The Comparative Analysis of Organisations', in March (ed.) 1965, pp. 678–709.

WARNER, W. L., and P. S. LUNT, 1941 *The Social Life of a Modern Community*, New Haven: Yale University Press.

WEBER, M., 1948 *From Max Weber* (ed. Girth, H., and C. W. Mills), London: Routledge and Kegan Paul.

WHITE, H. C., 1963 *An Anatomy of Kinship*, Englewood Cliffs, New Jersey: Prentice-Hall.

WHYTE, M. F., 1955 *Street Corner Society*, Chicago: University of Chicago Press.

WILDER, R. L., 1968 *Evolution of Mathematical Concepts: An Elementary Study*, New York: Wiley.

WILLER, D., 1967 *Scientific Sociology*, Englewood Cliffs: New Jersey, Prentice-Hall.

YASUDA, S., 1964 'A Methodological Inquiry into Social Mobility', *American Sociological Review*, Vol. 24, (February), pp. 16–23 and 'Reply to Gross', *American Sociological Review*, Vol. 24, pp. 887–8.

ZETTERBERG, Hans L., 1964 *On Theory and Verification in Sociology*, Totowa, New Jersey: The Bedminster Press.

Author Index

Subject Index

Social status, 105–19; formal representation of 109, and mobility, 120–22, objective, 107, systems, 119–20, subjective, 107

Social theory, axiomatised, 151–2

Status chains, 110, commutative diagrams, of, 114, isomorphism, of, 110, 112, representation of, 114

Status dimensions, 108, *see also* stratification characteristics; causal priority of, 118, diffuse, 115, ordering of, 117, relation between, 113

Status inheritance, 136

Status, symbols, 115

Stratification, 105–8, 120–1; characteristic (stratification variable), 108, preference order on stratification characteristic, 110, multidimensional theories of, 106–7, perception of, 104–5, 110–11, 118

Structural balance, *see* balance

Structure, 38–64; definition of, 38, compound, 41, indices of, 59–63, matrix, 43–4, multiple compound, 41, multiple simple, 41, simple, 41, task-precedence, 90–92, total, 41, total compound, 41

Structure theorems, 71–8

Sociogram, 43

Subset, 10

Superordinate, 98, least common, 98

Symmetric difference of sets, 12

Theories, sociological, 4, 8

Tree, 98

Triad, balanced, 66

Uniformity, 111

Union of sets, 11

Units of analysis, 2–3

Unit formation, 65–6, 69–70

Universal set (Universe), 11

Variables, 3, 10, 14–15

Vector, 166

Vulnerable organisational structure, 99

Venn diagram, 13

Work unit, 96, 104